THE
INFUSED
COCKTAIL HANDBOOK

THE
INFUSED
COCKTAIL HANDBOOK

THE ESSENTIAL GUIDE TO CREATING
YOUR OWN SIGNATURE SPIRITS AND BLENDS

KURT MAITLAND
AUTHOR OF *DRINK*

CIDER MILL
PRESS

BOOK
PUBLISHERS

CONTENTS

FOREWORD
INFUSIONS:
THE ART OF PLANNING AHEAD

BY ADAM SACHS

I'm not really a cocktail person.

I will admit that the foreword to a thoughtful book about making cocktails might not seem like the ideal forum for this particular admission. (I can see Kurt, my friend, and the author, down the bar, slightly choking on his smooth dram of Yamazaki single malt.)

Let me explain: I like *drinking* cocktails very much. I love going to cocktail bars, talking to bartenders, and watching them work. I like the martial precision, the lingo, the gleaming glassware and gear, the attention to detail. I just suffer from extremely boring tastes, cocktail-wise. Wherever I've been an established regular, they know me as the guy who always orders a Manhattan. Occasionally, I'll go crazy and have a gin Martini. I've got nothing against a bar with an avant-garde cocktail program (except maybe the use of the word "program" where "menu" would suffice). It's just that my tolerance for the booze outstrips my attention span for small-print menus and endlessly elaborate lists of ingredients.

But here's the thing: You don't have to be a habitué of hipster temples of haute mixology to benefit greatly from this ingenious book.

As you've likely gathered from the title, this is a book about infusions. The secret here is that infusions aren't just one more esoteric ingredient in inventive cocktail making. They're not another feather in the cap of the able home bartender. Instead they represent a whole new approach to creating distinct, unique, complex building blocks of deliciousness.

To infuse is to make something your own. Here we enter a realm that is closer to the world of cooking: the alchemy of turning everyday ingredients into something grander than the sum of their parts. And this is a subject I am happy to get deeply geeky about and appreciate in all its time-consuming, thought-provoking, guest-delighting, life-improving minutiae. I may not be a true cocktail connoisseur, but I'm a proud food nerd.

Seeing cocktails through the lens of infusions delights the committed kitchen tinkerer within. I subscribe to the motto of the late restaurateur and chef Judy Rogers who wrote in her iconic *Zuni Café Cookbook*: "Stop, think, there must be a harder way." The purpose of doing things the harder or the longer way isn't to wallow in needless suffering or to show off your prowess in the kitchen. The point is that there's payoff in the thinking and planning ahead. Yes, it takes three days to make the Zuni recipe for duck confit—but when you're done you've got this powerhouse of flavor in your cooking arsenal unlike any other, which you can then deploy in various guises and meals for weeks and months ahead.

It's the same with the infusions you'll learn from this group of very smart people Kurt's managed to gather together. Steep yourself in the art of infusing and you'll expand your range of creativity and what you can do from behind your home bar.

For the Sunflower Chartreuse Spritz, from London's Artesian bar (see page 254), we begin by cold infusing Chartreuse with toasted sunflower seeds. What is cold infusing but chilling? In other words, waiting around for the magic to happen. If humor = tragedy + time, then infusions are delicious, if unlikely, combinations of ingredients + time = mixology gold. Time is a crucial ingredient. Patience isn't just a virtue; with infusing, as with barbecue or any form of low and slow cooking, it's a superpower.

There's something about the investment of time, of learning to make the key ingredients rather than pulling them off the liquor store shelf, that satisfies a particular cooking and tinkering itch. Though I'm given to spending many hours making stock from scratch or tending to a hunk of meat soaking up smoke over glowing embers, when it comes time

to fix a drink I sometimes am too lazy to fetch the sweet vermouth from the fridge for a Manhattan and settle instead for bourbon on the rocks. That changed when last summer I spent some time making nocino, the bittersweet Italian digestif of neutral alcohol infused with green walnuts, sugar, and spices. After leaving it to rest for six months in a dark, cool place, I had something that wasn't just tasty: it was homemade, unique, all my own. Now I go out of my way to add a couple dashes of it to the bourbon for my own take on a Manhattan.

That's the other thing about making infusions: the bulk of the work is done upfront. Put in the time now to expand your tool kit of flavors, and when you're ready to shake or stir up a batch of cocktails for friends, the hard part is already behind you. The infusions you find here will not only help you become a more able host and creative drink maker, they'll streamline the process when it comes time to entertain. Best of all, you don't need a laundry list of exotic ingredients to make an interesting drink. Thanks to forethought and smart planning, you've already packed depth and complexity into these seemingly simple infusions of flavor.

Come to think of it, Kurt's book just may make a cocktail nerd of me yet.

INTRODUCTION

In the whisk(e)y world one often talks about "the" path they traveled as they learned more and more about various whiskies.

Some will hit a waypoint on that journey—let's say bourbon, Irish whiskey, or Scotch—and go no further, deciding instead to dig deeper and explore the nooks and crannies of a particular style or region. There's nothing wrong with that approach, as the main point of a journey through the spirit world is discovering what you like, and what you love.

I started with Jameson's Irish Whiskey, got into Maker's Mark, then Michter's, and I've recently been enamored with vintage Scotch, and Indian and Japanese whiskies. My curiosity has compelled me to keep moving, though in anything but a straight line.

My curiosity has kept me moving, which is how I went from whiskies into cocktails and from cocktails into a deeper niche within that world—infusions.

My previous book on cocktails (*Drink*, which Cider Mill Press released in 2019) is analogous to a general interest cookbook. This one is more focused, akin to a cookbook centered around soups, or Mexican cuisine, a deep dive into a developing style of cocktails that rely on infusions to provide their raison d'etre.

So, what's the deal with infusions, you might ask? When I asked my good friend, Michal Maziarz, who is currently serving as the bar manager at the Great Scotland Yard Hotel in London, about infusions, his response was sarcastic, but also very much to the point: "We do an amazing leaf infusion—it's called 'tea.'" What he is trying to say is that an infusion occurs any time a liquid solvent is used to extract a flavor. The resulting liquid will then be used as a vital component to the cocktails contained within. For our purposes, the extraction will generally be into an alcohol.

A few things before you start to dig in:

Most infusions take time. The cocktail itself will be quick to prepare, but for many of the recipes contained within, you will need to look at the recipes well ahead of time in order to acquire the ingredients required to make all of the components, and also factor in the amount of time needed to prepare the infusions. Shortchanging the infusing process will result in, shall we say, a less than optimal result.

If you're brand new to the world of infusing, I'd recommend that you start with some of the easier ones (such as the Mint-Infused Bourbon on page 51) and then make your way to the harder preparations. Perhaps you could partner up with a friend and taste your concoctions together, paying particular attention to the infusion prior to mixing the cocktail, as it is the piece that will make or break your drink. As with any craft, practice makes perfect, and you definitely want to have a few reps under your belt before you serve any of these up at a party.

Many of the bars providing these recipes make large batches of the infusions that they use, as they will turn to them over and over during the course of a week. Keep in mind that they will likely make more infusion-based cocktails in a day than you will in a month, and be careful about how much of the base infusion you make.

You will also want to be aware of how long the infusion will retain its flavor. This is less of an issue if you are infusing an entire bottle of liquor instead of making a shrub or a syrup, but it is always smart to keep notes on any infusion for reference in the future.

While most of the infusions and their methods of creation are pretty straightforward, a few of these infusion processes will be difficult to recreate in a standard home kitchen. Where possible these processes have been simplified. Truth be told, one of the bar owners told me that if they gave me the actual methods that they used to get one of their infusions, there was the possibility that an incident (perhaps an explosion) of some sort might occur. The cocktails included within fall well short of that level of excitement, but let's just say that you've been briefed on the degree of difficulty required to be on the cutting edge of the cocktail world.

To get back to the "journey" theme I began with, let us spend a moment discussing how I pulled this book together. This book really took shape in London. Of course. When I started to travel beyond North America and the Caribbean, London was the first place I visited. Why? First off, as I can only claim basic linguistic competence in one language (you got it, English), London was a good option. Years of watching British TV such as *Doctor Who*, *Monty Python*, *The Benny Hill Show*, etc. gave me a sense of the difference between American and English culture, and turned me into something of an Anglophile.

That initial trip led to many others, and the connections I made during these sojourns made London, circa 2019, a natural beginning for this book. (Commence name dropping—albeit it well deserved). Sukhinder Singh, co-owner of the Whisky Exchange, and owner of one of the world's truly great whisky collections, gave me a list of his favorite London cocktail bars. In the end, Sukhinder's recommendations led to at least half of the London bars included here, so we owe him and his excellent taste a big thanks.

One of the bars Sukhinder suggested was Artesian, which is located in the Langham Hotel. Gabriele Sasnauskaite was my bartender on my first trip, and she quickly opened my eyes to the incredible range infusions offer, serving me a Scotch-centered cocktail that was as clear as water, but oh so tasty. She also made me a Michter's & Pear (see page 44), a drink so incredible we just had to include it. Gabriele, an amazing bartender in her own right, also threw me a few valuable bar recommendations (quick tip: if a bartender tells you about bars that

they love, always find a way to get there). Her insights, advice, and skills helped me articulate what I was trying to do with this book, and I can't thank her enough.

Another memorable, and invaluable, stop during my tour of London was to Hide Below, where the talented Oskar Kinberg provided me with a few recipes, and a ton of insight by talking me through his process.

After my spin through London (and a quick trip to Scotland because ... whisky), I ended up in Hamburg, Germany, where I was lucky enough to have two world-class bars right near my hotel—Rabbithole and Drip Bar. Both are pushing innovative, infusion-heavy bar programs that ended up being an ideal fit for what I was hoping to do with this book, and both were kind enough to share their knowledge with me.

From there, I traveled to Belfast before heading back to NYC, and managed to make a brief trip down to New Orleans while wrapping up this manuscript.

Each stop had much to offer, and I've done my best to translate the excitement I felt as I made my way through this new realm.

All that is needed is one last ingredient—you.

On its own, a cocktail book is nothing more than a collection of thoughts, ideas, and suggestions. It is when you share and enjoy what you've learned with friends and family that it becomes something else. It becomes something you can savor over and over again—becomes more than words on a page. Knowing that makes a book like this a pleasure to write.

ARTESIAN, LONDON

Q & A WITH WILLIAM CAMPBELL-ROWNTREE, BAR SUPERVISOR

TELL US ABOUT THE GENERAL THEME OF YOUR BAR.

The bar does not have a strict theme as such. We are a five-star hotel bar working in central London. Oxford Street is on our doorstep and we are a short walk from everything you would want to see in London. However, we pride ourselves on being down to earth, offering great hospitality and drinks in a much more relaxed environment for a hotel bar. Our menu does have a theme, currently minimalism, as in the art form. We're focused on exploring the idea that less can be more, and how we can apply this to our drinks.

WHAT DO YOU LOOK FOR WHEN WORKING WITH OR CREATING INFUSIONS? HOW DO YOU USE THEM IN CREATING NEW COCKTAILS FOR YOUR MENU?

We, as a team, always ask ourselves: Is this practical? Is this the best way to do this? Will this give me the flavor and result that I need? I think asking yourself why you use certain techniques is very important and we are incredibly lucky to have a lab and the tools at our disposal so that we can do almost anything. However, it is not always necessary to use a technical piece of equipment—you really have to look at what you want and are trying to do with those flavors and infusions.

DO YOU HAVE A FAVORITE SPIRIT TO WORK WITH WHEN MAKING INFUSIONS?

When creating infusions you want something that is going to really carry the flavor and make it shine through. Vodka, or any neutral-grain spirit, is going to be the best option to take on flavor. Although we also use simple water to infuse our flavors, it all depends on the ingredients and how hard it will be to extract that flavor. However, we do have an abundance of whisky distillate in the lab, and I know a few members of the team have been testing some tinctures and bitters with that, as it is just so potent!

WHAT IS THE HARDEST PART OF WORKING WITH INFUSIONS? ARE THERE ANY DOWNSIDES TO WORKING WITH INFUSION-BASED COCKTAILS RELATIVE TO OTHER COCKTAILS?

There are definitely some downsides and things you have to be aware of and look out for. Consistency, especially with fresh and/or soft fruits and vegetables. Ingredients, like seasons, change. Even when stored in a fridge for one week the sugar and acid levels of some fruits can change drastically. So, when doing cold infusions that take a long time, you have to be very careful. That's why we balance our syrups and cordials with acids and will check Brix levels (the percentage of sugar or water-soluble content) if the ingredients are being really troublesome. This is where the more technical equipment becomes the star of the show, because it takes a huge risk factor out of the creation of some of the drinks.

CAN YOU TAKE US THROUGH THE PROCESS YOU USE TO MAKE SOME OF YOUR INFUSIONS? IN PARTICULAR, I'M INTERESTED IN LEARNING MORE ABOUT YOUR LAB—HOW YOU BUILT IT, HOW YOU USE IT, ETC.

The lab is the hero of our bar, and we are also very lucky in that we get to show guests the area. Our lab is a space on the lower level where all of our prep is done, with one staff member there for 10 hours each day. All infusions, blending, and batching happens in this area, along with ice prep for cocktails and service, ordering, deliveries, stock, etc. It's a tough job that requires organization, hard work, and knowledge. In the lab we have all our ingredients, induction hob, dehydrator, sous vide and bain marie, theromix, rotovap, and centrifuge. We are incredibly lucky! We center our use of the lab on creating and maximizing flavors we use, and the hope that all the hard work behind the scenes creates a magical moment for guests.

IF INFUSIONS ARE JUST ONE PHASE IN THE DEVELOPMENT OF COCKTAILS, DO YOU HAVE ANY THOUGHTS ON WHAT COMES NEXT?

Infusions for us are not a step in the development of a drink, but an option you must consider in all elements of drink creation. It is learning and discovering the best way to highlight a flavor. Although there are many other fantastic ways in which to do that, infusions are one of the most effective.

HIDE BELOW, LONDON

Q & A WITH OSKAR KINBERG, HEAD BARTENDER

TELL US A BIT ABOUT HOW YOUR BAR GOT STARTED AND HOW YOU GOT INTO THE BUSINESS.

Hide Below is situated under Hide restaurant, a collaboration between Hedonism Wines' Evgeny Chichvarkin, Tatiana Fokina, and chef Ollie Dabbous. The bar program is designed by me, Oskar Kinberg,

and I'm a bartender. Like many other bartenders, I had seen the movie *Cocktail* and was drawn to the profession.

TELL US ABOUT THE GENERAL THEME OF YOUR BAR AND WHAT ROLE INFUSIONS PLAY IN YOUR COCKTAIL PROGRAM.

Hide Below prides itself on using the best ingredients available during the peak of their seasonality and turning them into delicious cocktails. We also offer an extensive wine list with over 6,500 references by the bottle, alongside a selection of fine and rare spirits from all over the world. If you feel lost having to reckon with such a large selection, our team of friendly sommeliers and bartenders are more than happy to guide you through our various menus and offer advice.

WHAT DO YOU LOOK FOR WHEN WORKING WITH OR CREATING INFUSIONS? HOW DO YOU USE THEM IN CREATING NEW COCKTAILS FOR YOUR MENU?

To get a result that resembles the original as closely as possible. Also, see my response to the final question.

WHAT IS THE HARDEST PART OF WORKING WITH INFUSIONS? ARE THERE ANY DOWNSIDES TO WORKING WITH INFUSION-BASED COCKTAILS RELATIVE TO OTHER COCKTAILS?

Any time you work with homemade ingredients consistency is the hardest thing to get right. You want every guest to have the same great experience. That's why recipes need to be very exact, down to the milligram in some cases, and then followed as meticulously. Fruits and herbs also change their flavor and color depending on the time of year. Sometimes from day-to-day. That, too, needs to be taken into consideration when infusing. If two plums taste very different, it might be worth doing a batch with 20 plums to get a fairer representation of the flavor. This way you guard yourself against any odd ones, and hopefully it won't be too much of a difference between batches.

CAN YOU TALK US THROUGH THE PROCESS YOU USE TO MAKE SOME OF YOUR INFUSIONS?

Some ingredients benefit from being heated, in which case we put them, along with the liquid they go with, into a vacuum bag and cook them sous vide at a suitable temperature for that ingredient. Others taste better when not cooked. I avoid heating up fruits, as they become jammy and lose their freshness. Spices, teas, and types of wood benefit from heating up, and we normally do this in a sous vide. Main reason for this is that it is easier to control the temperature. Being able to control the temperature in a sealed bag also ensures we don't lose any of the alcohol or liquid, other than what gets soaked up in the fruit, zest, wood, tea, etc.

IF INFUSIONS ARE JUST ONE PHASE IN THE DEVELOPMENT OF COCKTAILS, DO YOU HAVE ANY THOUGHTS ON WHAT COMES NEXT?

The way I normally work is to have a clear image in my head of what the finished cocktail will be. Although the method is secondary, it often includes infusing something into something along the way. For example, with the cocktail Adam & Eve, I wanted to highlight fig leaf as an ingredient. Fig leaf is really fragrant and has a coconut note to it. So I based the flavors around that. In order to get consistency between the cocktails, I opted to infuse a set amount of fig leaf into a mix of rum and cider brandy. This makes it more exact than muddling or shaking with the leaf *a la minute* (prepared to order), which in a way is an infusion, too. This is a normal cold infusion that doesn't require any heat, you simply leave the leaves in the alcohol and let them soak until the liquor has been infused to the preferred strength. Then comes the adding of other flavors. I knew I wanted this drink to be a milk punch, so I wanted flavors that go well with dairy, such as spices, nuts, etc. I ended up adding Fino sherry and Falernum. As a whole, the fig leaf really comes through and the other flavors complement it. This is how I typically make drinks. One star ingredient, with others around it to make it taste even better.

If you're looking for more information on how Oskar makes cocktails, I strongly recommend his *Cocktail Cookbook.*

COUPETTE, LONDON

Q & A WITH ANDRE MARCU, BAR MANAGER

TELL US A BIT ABOUT HOW YOUR BAR GOT STARTED AND HOW YOU GOT INTO THE BUSINESS.

After launching in June 2017, Coupette soon became known for its authenticity and unpretentious style. It has since gained an international reputation, winning the industry's top awards and accolades, and has successfully retained its place in the 2019 "World's Best Bars" list.

At Coupette we have always prioritized results over techniques. Each of our drinks are presented in beautiful, classic glassware and consciously balanced for simplicity and discovery. Complex ideas and lengthy procedures take place behind the scenes rather than as showy garnishes. This leaves our guests free to explore the flavors and nuances of the cocktail through drinking it, rather than depending on elaborate serves and extended explanations.

TELL US ABOUT THE GENERAL THEME OF YOUR BAR AND WHAT ROLE INFUSIONS PLAY IN YOUR COCKTAIL PROGRAM.

We are a French-inspired neighborhood bar, and we use infusions regularly in our drinks. Although we are not a very high-tech prep bar, we are very inspired by classic French cooking, and cooking in general, where the main goal is enhancing layers of flavors through different techniques. Infusion always played a massive role in our cocktail program, as we have lots of infused ingredients on our current menu, and

we believe we have managed to master our infusion techniques over time.

WHAT DO YOU LOOK FOR WHEN WORKING WITH OR CREATING INFUSIONS? HOW DO YOU USE THEM IN CREATING NEW COCKTAILS FOR YOUR MENU?

I am always looking at what results I want to achieve, and I find that infusions create the bind between flavors, as well as enhancing each on their own. I always use an infusion for the "big bang" flavor (that's what I call it!), which stands for that main flavor which lasts from start to finish, and every other flavor just spins around.

DO YOU HAVE A FAVORITE SPIRIT TO WORK WITH WHEN MAKING YOUR INFUSIONS?

I think every spirit has its own character when it comes to infusions. I am always thinking of a spirit base as a platform on which I can build the drink and reach my goals in terms of flavor. At the moment I am working a lot with Calvados and brown flavors. One of my favorites is Calvados infused with burned butter. Absolutely delicious.

WHAT IS THE HARDEST PART OF WORKING WITH INFUSIONS? ARE THERE ANY DOWNSIDES TO WORKING WITH INFUSION-BASED COCKTAILS RELATIVE TO OTHER COCKTAILS?

Timings and temperatures. Timings are very important when we talk about infusions. Once you have developed an exact recipe and you follow it each and every time, you'll be fine. The only downside I can possibly see would be the wait-to-infuse time. But that is only if you don't have an organized enough mise en place.

THE COCKTAIL TRADING COMPANY, LONDON

Q & A WITH ELLIOT BALL, CO-OWNER

TELL US ABOUT HOW YOUR BAR GOT STARTED AND HOW YOU GOT INTO THE BUSINESS.

CTC was founded by three of us—Andy Milz, Olly Brading, and myself—we all approached the hospitality industry from very different backgrounds; I come from a neuroscience background. An obsession with understanding the brain's interpretation and construction of flavor were at the foundation of the drinks. Olly's background in music fed into a deep understanding of atmosphere, and Andy, who flung himself straight at bar management laughably young, contributed a profound feel for operations and unified the concept.

TELL US ABOUT THE GENERAL THEME OF YOUR BAR AND WHAT ROLE INFUSIONS PLAY IN YOUR COCKTAIL PROGRAM.

So there isn't a theme, per se—given the name, everyone knows we're cocktail-focused, so from there, we simply tried to make everything as warm and welcoming as possible, which yielded a particularly obvious design aesthetic—classic British pub, where all are welcome. Basically, we loathe any kind of exclusivity in bars. As for infusions, like most,

we initially used them for imbuing flavors into liquids already in use—flavoring spirits, herbal teas, etc. In more recent menus, we've been using them more for mouthfeel, however.

WHAT DO YOU LOOK FOR WHEN WORKING WITH OR CREATING INFUSIONS? HOW DO YOU USE THEM IN CREATING NEW COCKTAILS FOR YOUR MENU?

This is where lots of people are going to start talking about quality of ingredients—that's undeniably important, but our thing at CTC has always been hitting quality whilst ensuring consistency at high volume—we're fortunate enough to be a pretty packed place most of the time, so things need to be achievable quickly and consistently. So we're fans of Occam's Razor—the simplest of two equivalent outcomes is best. For the Five Grape Long Island (see page 300), for example, the tea infusion was: a) fairly unique; b) very straightforward; c) consistent across different times due to cold infusion; and d) factored in the necessary dilution in preparing the drink in advance, allowing for carbonation and batching.

DO YOU HAVE A FAVORITE SPIRIT TO WORK WITH WHEN MAKING YOUR INFUSIONS?

No particular favorites—while infusing into spirits does produce different outcomes than water, a key part of the benefit is in not altering dilution by going directly to the base product. So if it works in the base you're intending for that drink, dandy. However, I'd imagine we infuse clear spirits more, as do most, partly because they tend to benefit from the added complexity and mouthfeel most, and partly because heavily infusing vodka, for example, with your chosen ingredient essentially creates a tincture that can be used without adding much in the way of booze/dilution.

WHAT IS THE HARDEST PART OF WORKING WITH INFUSIONS? ARE THERE ANY

DOWNSIDES TO WORKING WITH INFUSION-BASED COCKTAILS?

Consistency, as I've said, is hugely important to us, and there's a lot that can go wrong, though things become easier with strict operations and guidelines. Even just labeling things correctly to ensure they aren't stored in the wrong place or infused for the incorrect amount of time. Beyond that, consistency of ingredients—the classic difference is between ground and loose-leaf tea, which will produce very different outcomes in both character and overall quality. And then there are the effects of getting the same product from two different suppliers! Not to mention the ground mace that's sold around the world as nutmeg ...

DRIP BAR, HAMBURG, GERMANY

Q & A WITH CHRISTIAN JANZEN, OWNER

TELL US A BIT ABOUT HOW YOUR BAR GOT STARTED AND HOW YOU GOT INTO THE BUSINESS.

Everything started with a self-made cold brew dripper, dripping rum through gingerbread and making a Gingerbread Daquiri. After figuring out several recipes, I opened Drip Bar shortly after.

TELL US ABOUT THE GENERAL THEME OF YOUR BAR AND WHAT ROLE INFUSIONS PLAY IN YOUR COCKTAIL PROGRAM.

Our bar is a hidden speakeasy in Hamburg. The theme behind Drip Bar is to infuse our spirits with the help of cold brew drippers, which are generally used to make a Japanese-style, cold-infused coffee. The cocktail menu is inside a fairytale book, where only drip cocktails are listed. Let's say, for example, a 10-year-old rum is dripping for 72 hours slowly through salty peanuts. With this salty peanut rum we are creating a Salty Peanut Old Fashioned, which contains rum, maple syrup, orange bitters, and aromatic bitters.

WHAT DO LOOK FOR WHEN WORKING WITH AND CREATING INFUSIONS? HOW DO YOU USE THEM IN CREATING NEW COCKTAILS FOR YOUR MENU?

When creating a new cocktail, we take a classic cocktail, think about the different aromas it has, and then try to add an unexpected aroma to one of the spirits.

DO YOU HAVE A FAVORITE SPIRIT TO WORK WITH WHEN MAKING YOUR INFUSIONS?

Not really. We like to work with all different kinds of spirits, to challenge ourselves.

WHAT IS THE HARDEST PART OF WORKING WITH INFUSIONS? ARE THERE ANY DOWNSIDES TO WORKING WITH INFUSION-BASED COCKTAILS RELATIVE TO OTHER COCKTAILS?

The hardest part is to organize all of the dripped spirits to ensure that we never run out of stock. The dripping time lasts at least 24 hours and can go for up to 72 hours. All of the effort is definitely worth it, for what we get out of natural aromas.

THE RABBITHOLE, HAMBURG, GERMANY

Q & A WITH CONSTANZE LAY, OWNER

TELL US A BIT ABOUT HOW YOUR BAR GOT STARTED AND HOW YOU GOT INTO THE BUSINESS.

I started The Rabbithole March 2016. My way into the business was the classical one: while studying I worked as a waiter. Before I could do my exams at university I had a little time so I did the IHK Barmeister at the Barschule Rostock (Germany). After finishing university, I had the chance to build up a bar for people who had a room but no experience. I made the concept, formed the team, chose the liquors, and wrote and calculated the menu. It worked out very well and was fun, so I decided not to look for a job in the field I studied, but for an opportunity to build up my bar.

TELL US ABOUT THE GENERAL THEME OF YOUR BAR AND WHAT ROLE INFUSIONS PLAY IN YOUR COCKTAIL PROGRAM.

The general theme of our bar is our special cocktail creations, and infusions play a big role here. We twist classics and also create totally new drinks (as far as we know). We have 24 drinks on our menu, and 10 of the drinks contain infused liquors.

WHAT DO YOU LOOK FOR WHEN WORKING WITH OR CREATING INFUSIONS? HOW DO YOU USE THEM IN CREATING NEW COCKTAILS FOR YOUR MENU?

Normally I look for something new, a spirit that is not buyable. Most of the time when we have an idea for a drink with a special taste, we try several ways, like using fresh ingredients, turning it into a syrup, or doing an infusion with it.

DO YOU HAVE A FAVORITE SPIRIT TO WORK WITH WHEN MAKING YOUR INFUSIONS?

Most of the spirits we use for infusions are not aged in barrels, like gin, vodka, mezcal, or blanco tequila. But we have also worked with bourbon and aged rum, and with liqueurs.

WHAT IS THE HARDEST PART OF WORKING WITH INFUSIONS? ARE THERE ANY DOWNSIDES TO WORKING WITH INFUSION-BASED COCKTAILS RELATIVE TO OTHER COCKTAILS?

The only downside I can see in our bar is that we spend a lot of time for our mise en place, because the infusion process takes a lot of time. And of course you need to buy the stuff you need, like a cold dripper, sous vide, bottles. And we have the same problem with every homemade item: you risk running out of it on a long and heavy weekend night. You have to figure out a system to constantly reproduce the mise en place. And working with fresh ingredients means you always have to check the amount you need to reproduce the same taste.

CAN YOU TALK US THROUGH THE PROCESS YOU USE TO MAKE SOME OF YOUR INFUSIONS?

With the cold dripper we infuse gin with lavender and gin with Earl Grey tea. The spirit drips through the botanical, taking the aroma but not the bitter parts.

With sous vide we infuse gin with cilantro, (4 cups gin with 3 cups cilantro leaves), tequila with arugula (4 cups tequila with 1 cup arugula), and tequila with fennel (4 cups tequila with 2 cups chopped fennel). With sous vide we freeze the botanicals before to intensify the aroma. We vacuum seal it and cook it at 140°F for 45 minutes. We also do the base of our homemade Falernum with sous vide: we vacuum-seal overproof rum with spices, ginger, and lime twists.

For our cardamom vodka, we macerate crushed cardamom seeds in vodka for 3 days. For our cheese bourbon, we macerate Comté cheese and pineapple shell in bourbon for 4 weeks.

SUGAR MONK, HARLEM

Q & A WITH EKTORAS BINIKOS, CO-FOUNDER & PARTNER

TELL US ABOUT HOW YOUR BAR GOT STARTED AND HOW YOU GOT INTO THE BUSINESS.

I arrived in the US at the age of 21, from Greece. I came to study. I wanted to supplement my income by doing something that I believed paid well. So, I began working at a restaurant as a bar back. I thought it would make the most sense to get involved in this particular business, coming from Greece where my parents were involved in the hospitality industry and were also amateur distillers. Soon enough, I decided to attend a school for bartending and became a bartender very fast after that. The rest is history.

My life partner and business associate, Simon Jutras, and I moved to Harlem about seven years ago. We love the neighborhood and thought of doing something locally that paid tribute to the history of Harlem's past—more specifically, the early speakeasys of the Harlem Renaissance.

TELL US ABOUT THE GENERAL THEME OF YOUR BAR AND WHAT ROLE INFUSIONS PLAY IN YOUR COCKTAIL PROGRAM.

Sugar Monk is a speakeasy geared toward the art of mixology. We have a vision of a forward-thinking and sophisticated place where neighborhood residents, cocktail aficionados, foreign visitors, and the arts community will all gather.

Obviously, infusions play a very important part in our beverage program, in that they create a base for innovative cocktails that transcend the senses.

WHAT DO YOU LOOK FOR WHEN WORKING WITH OR CREATING INFUSIONS? HOW DO YOU USE THEM IN CREATING NEW COCKTAILS FOR YOUR MENU?

Every cocktail is a journey. Infusions bring different flavors—the sense of other cultures and living beings, and they take you on a journey to other living worlds. More specifically, I love to use spices that stem from culinary traditions that are utilized in various parts of the globe. It's another way of communicating between cultures, and something that I find to be very exciting and thrilling.

DO YOU HAVE A FAVORITE SPIRIT TO WORK WITH WHEN MAKING YOUR INFUSIONS?

Yes, I do. I love the way aquavit takes on infusions. It is this earthy spirit that almost shocks all flavors and mutates them through its spices in wonderful ways. One of my favorite infusions with aquavit is with baharat, which is a mixture of various Moroccan spices (see page 286).

WHAT IS THE HARDEST PART OF WORKING WITH INFUSIONS? ARE THERE ANY DOWNSIDES TO WORKING WITH INFUSION-BASED COCKTAILS RELATIVE TO OTHER COCKTAILS?

Timing is very important when it comes to infusions. You must experiment and go through several trials in order to find the perfect timing that creates the best infusion. You don't want to produce something that is over- or under-infused.

The downside of working with infusion-based cocktails is that you must go through the infusions very fast. Infusions still retain particles no matter the multiple straining process that, if not completed in a timely manner, can affect the taste and flavor. At Sugar Monk we go through our infusions rather fast (making small batches helps) so that there is a consistency regarding the exact flavor profile of our infused cocktails.

CAN YOU TAKE US THROUGH THE PROCESS YOU USE TO MAKE SOME OF YOUR INFUSIONS?

First phase is research. I will visit various spice stores and markets searching for interesting things to use. I buy samples and then I try to infuse different spirits with them in order to see which one works best with the spice, dry fruit, or even bark. It's all chemistry. Like the way perfume will react to your skin or synthesize with your skin and reflect the aroma. Then there is, of course, the ratio and the timing. You need to experiment a lot to establish the best possible combination of factors. From that point on you will start building your cocktail based on the concept you have in your head. Upon that process sometimes you must go back and make some adjustments to your infusion.

IF INFUSIONS ARE JUST ONE PHASE IN THE DEVELOPMENT OF COCKTAILS, WHAT DO YOU SEE FOR THE FUTURE?

I think the future in our cocktailian work lays the path toward semiochemical messengers. What I mean is that for all of us humans the sense of smell sometimes can take a twist towards some mystical connotations. Our subconscious memory can be stored with unexpected vividness for a long time and when re-experienced these moments can evoke strong, sudden emotions. Think of the possibilities of synthesized molecules added to a concoction to take you on a journey around the world, visiting places that you only dreamed of and that will stay forever in your olfactory mind.

DIAMOND DOGS, QUEENS

Q & A WITH NICK ELEZOVIC

My brother John and I have been in the food and beverage industry most of our adult lives. I had been in the hotel field for close to 15 years as of 2011. I was also moonlighting at my local—the Sparrow Tavern in Astoria—when he came to visit one late night after his gig as bar manager/bartender at the now defunct Revival bar near Union Square. He shared the idea that we could do just as good of a job as the people we worked for, if not better, if we had a bar of our own. Intrigued, I set aside my ambitions as a film editor to undertake and conquer the world of bureaucracy and red tape involved with opening a bar in New York City, a stressful undertaking that nearly did us in several times. But we did it, and we haven't looked back.

The name Diamond Dogs was originally going to be a cocktail name. But the more I thought about it, the more I liked it as a bar name. Growing up in NYC, I spent most of my years in the East Village and on the Lower East Side going to all the record shops. But I did remember occasionally going to West Bleecker Street to a record shop called Rebel Rebel (also named after a David Bowie song). I would go to Rebel Rebel if there was a hard-to-find CD of some British rock band I was obsessed with at the time. It dawned on me: If there could be a record shop called Rebel Rebel, why can't we have a bar called Diamond Dogs?

TELL US ABOUT THE GENERAL THEME OF YOUR BAR.

Dark, sexy, rock 'n' roll neighborhood bar with unfussy yet creative cocktails, a solid rotating beer selection, and the best music. We wanted to open a bar that we would want to go to all the time, that felt like the bars of the Lower East Side during the early to mid-90s that we grew up going to, as well as some of the Brooklyn bars from the mid-90s to early 2000s.

WHAT DO YOU LOOK FOR WHEN WORKING WITH OR CREATING INFUSIONS? HOW DO YOU USE THEM IN CREATING NEW COCKTAILS FOR YOUR MENU?

Trying to find complementary flavors to whatever spirits we want to have fun with, as our infusion ideas are usually pretty random. We always try to keep in mind the seasonality of the ingredients of the drink in progress. We are suckers for teas, and sometimes it is a crutch we have trouble moving on from. But the results have been extremely pleasing, and we as well as our customers have very much enjoyed the results.

DO YOU HAVE A FAVORITE SPIRIT TO WORK WITH WHEN MAKING YOUR INFUSIONS?

Agave-based spirits are wonderful to work with, and chamomile always shines in them.

WHAT IS THE HARDEST PART OF WORKING WITH INFUSIONS? ARE THERE ANY DOWNSIDES TO WORKING WITH INFUSION-BASED COCKTAILS RELATIVE TO OTHER COCKTAILS?

Taking the chamomile as an example—it has been difficult for us to get accurate portions to measure out for infusions, as we use whole chamomile flowers from the spice shops in New York as opposed to using tea bags. The vast width of different

flavor profiles and characteristics of all the styles of agave-based spirits make it difficult to use a standard measurement of chamomile to infuse across the board. We had to resort to just making a chamomile syrup to dial up and down the amounts used to complement that particular style of mezcal. Occasionally, you can make decent-to-borderline great drinks with a well tequila (only if it is 100 percent agave).

Using chamomile and a pinch of salt will separate the pretenders from the midrange to higher-quality agave spirits, which will make for much better cocktails.

CAN YOU TALK US THROUGH THE PROCESS YOU USE TO MAKE SOME OF YOUR INFUSIONS?

Most recently, we started spicing our bourbon for our seasonal hot apple cider, instead of spicing the cider itself. It became very messy and too inconsistent to spice the cider in the kettle as it warms up, only to be replenished with fresh cider that has to wait to be infused with spices as it is replenished. Our spice-infused bourbon (see page 52) not only makes it much easier on the staff to get consistent flavor every time, but now we have a delicious alternative to Fireball for all the weekend, amateur-hour drinkers looking for a cheap, quick fix before moving on to other shenanigans.

TRAVEL BAR, BROOKLYN

Q & A WITH MICHAEL VACHERESSE

TELL US A BIT ABOUT HOW YOUR BAR GOT STARTED AND HOW YOU GOT INTO THE BUSINESS.

Let's start with Travel Bar. We are located in Brooklyn and we pride ourselves on being an under-the-radar cocktail bar. Our cocktails are simple—no more than three ingredients, but these ingredients are often infused with a different element. But more than that, with more than 35 cocktails, many of them infused, we love to understand what people who are new to the bar like, and introduce them to new things. I have been doing that my whole career in bartending, whether it is at an American standard like Gotham Bar & Grill or Masa, the five-star Japanese restaurant.

TELL US ABOUT THE GENERAL THEME OF YOUR BAR AND WHAT ROLE INFUSIONS PLAY IN YOUR BAR PROGRAM.

Our whole emphasis is providing a bar program that is expertly crafted, in a neighborhood where that is unexpected, and in an environment that is comfortable. At our heart, we are a local bar. Infusions play a big role in our bar program because it allows us control exactly how much of an ingredient is in any one of our cocktails. It allows us to expertly craft our cocktails, which is what we are all about.

WHAT DO YOU LOOK FOR WHEN WORKING WITH OR CREATING INFUSIONS? HOW DO

YOU USE THEM IN CREATING NEW COCKTAILS FOR YOUR MENU?

It's a lot of experimentation. I have a rolodex of sorts in my head and I am at the point where I can instantly recognize if flavors will go well together. I have done oddball ones that I love, but have been reluctant to make them public. But when world-class bartenders come in, I ask them to come behind the bar and make a drink on the spot. I asked Damon Boelte [of Brooklyn's Grand Army bar] and Thomas Waugh [the beverage director for New York's celebrated Major Food Group] to make a cocktail with a gin that was fat-washed in truffle oil. It was fun to watch where it took them. They both went in completely different directions.

DO YOU HAVE A FAVORITE SPIRIT TO WORK WITH WHEN MAKING YOUR INFUSIONS?

I work with gin the most because it has a number of personalities. If you work with a neutral grain spirit, like a vodka, the only flavor you are going to pull is the infusing element. If I want that, then I will make a syrup.

WHAT IS THE HARDEST PART OF WORKING WITH INFUSIONS? ARE THERE ANY DOWNSIDES TO WORKING WITH INFUSION-BASED COCKTAILS RELATIVE TO OTHER COCKTAILS?

Shelf stabilization is definitely a downside, as is timing on production and inventory.

CAN YOU TALK US THROUGH THE PROCESS YOU USE TO MAKE SOME OF YOUR INFUSIONS?

It's a lot of experimentation, and I am willing to lose the inventory and space to get the right infusion, which is a big deal since Brooklyn bars are tight on profit margin and space. Most of the time, I make batches and I know fairly quickly if it is going to work. But then again, I have had blackberries sitting in gin for the past 14 months in our basement.

IF INFUSIONS ARE JUST ONE PHASE IN THE DEVELOPMENT OF COCKTAILS, DO YOU HAVE ANY THOUGHTS ON WHAT COMES NEXT?

Syrups. They are much cheaper to experiment with. All you need is sugar, glass jars, and time. The possible ingredients are endless. It would be best to start flavoring ice teas or lemonade, but you can quickly move to cocktails.

BABEL, BELFAST

Q & A WITH FRANCIS COSGROVE, ASSISTANT MANAGER

TELL US A BIT ABOUT HOW YOUR BAR GOT STARTED AND HOW YOU GOT INTO THE BUSINESS?

Babel, the rooftop bar, situated atop of the Bullitt Hotel, came about as a product of Belfast's wants and needs. It has been noted in recent years that Belfast is rapidly developing—so much so that it is now nipping on the heels of other, much more developed European capital cities. It was a small city but with high expectations! As such, there was a place in the market for a craft cocktail bar with a cosmopolitan ambiance, focused on delivering quality service alongside quality drinks.

Personally, my interest in the beverage market started when I was rejected from a teaching course (midlife crisis!). A lot of people are empathetic when they hear this; however, looking back I have no regrets. The creativity, freedom, and community that hospitality (in particular, the bar trade) has offered are things which I feel can't be offered in any other sector. To me, hospitality has become a most favorable profession which has allowed me to go from strength to strength.

TELL US ABOUT THE GENERAL THEME OF YOUR BAR AND WHAT ROLE INFUSIONS PLAY IN YOUR COCKTAIL PROGRAM.

At Babel, we are focused on consistently delivering an excellent level of drinks for all of our consumers. It's a goal which has paid off, as it has now become a destination for cocktail aficionados. Regarding infusions, they are viewed as a method to help enhance the flavor of a drink. We use a lot of homemade ingredients—particularly shrubs and syrups. A few of these include a Chili & Mango Shrub (see page 207), a Basil & Honey Syrup (see page 86), and a Sage & Stout Syrup. Each ingredient relies on a different infusion method in order to extract the desired flavor. For example, we begin our Chili & Mango Shrub by leaving red chili and fresh mango to sit in apple cider vinegar for a few days, whereas with the Basil & Honey Syrup we opt for a sous-vide method to extract as much flavor as possible. This allows us to proper utilize the end result on our drinks menu.

WHAT DO YOU LOOK FOR WHEN CREATING NEW INFUSIONS? HOW DO YOU USE THEM IN CREATING NEW COCKTAILS FOR YOUR MENU?

When it comes to infusions, the main thing I look for is flavor. I want to ensure the infusion will create a flavorsome syrup or spirit that can work well as a stand-alone drink or as an enhancing ingredient. There are a multitude of ways you can utilize infusions.

Most recently, I have been looking at different milk punches, which has been exciting. I created a Banana Water Milk Punch, which was inspired by Jack Wareing of Porter's Gin. It was created by infusing Boatyard Vodka with banana peels, creating a banana water, combining the two together, and adding citrus and hot milk to clarify. It was one of the most exciting drinks I have created recently. The infusion of banana peels amplified the banana flavor already present in the Boatyard, but also allowed me to utilize an ingredient that would otherwise be discarded.

When it comes to using infusions as enhancers, I consider how I want the final drink to taste. I also like to consider which spirits will be used. One drink on our menu is a twist on the classic Whiskey Sour which uses Powers whiskey as its base. In my opinion, as a pot-still whiskey, Powers tends to be more full-bodied, carry tannins, and have a bolder nature compared to other whiskeys on the market. With this in mind, we have created a simple tea syrup which really complements the pot-still character to create a more rounded final product.

I don't really have a favorite—the spirits world is so diverse. I tend to consider how a flavor is going to work in a drink rather than considering which spirit I want to base a drink around.

However, vodka, of course, works well. As a neutral spirit, it really allows the flavors of the ingredients used in the infusion to shine. Some people may find this very one-dimensional and simplistic. However, if you're just starting off, or if your goal is to extract a singular flavor, it's perfect! If opting for a tincture, I tend to go with Wray & Nephew rum. As an overproof rum, it has always been amazing for extracting flavors, and I've yet to experience an unpleasant end result! This could, however, be a biased comment, as I fell in love with Wray & Nephew after my first Nuclear Daiquiri.

Having made bitters previously, I found that Everclear rectified spirit worked well. As the end result is normally applied in dashes, the extra flavor extracted due to the high ABV of Everclear allowed for a punchier end result. This helps the flavors come through in the end drink. Long story short, depending on what my end goal is, my base spirit for an infusion is likely to change.

I think sometimes the idea of infusing spirits can be daunting. For example, if you have a beautiful bottle of Cognac that you are intending to flavor, it can be daunting that the end results may not turn out well! However, there are certainly more positives than negatives. The ability to add complexity and depth to a drink through infusions far outweighs the risk of wastage. Additionally, despite how an infusion ends up, you can always find a use for it—I don't know how many times I have walked into a bar and seen a special being promoted due to an infusion which didn't work as planned!

I've already touched briefly on a banana milk punch I made before. It was one of my favorite drinks to make and I was extremely proud of how it turned out. It was quite technical, yet extremely simple to make. Most importantly, it was flavorsome! Again, I have to thank Jack for talking me through how to make a "banana water." We then got talking about its multiple uses and how it could be used to create a liqueur or a wine. However, after chatting to a close friend, I wanted to see if it would work as a milk punch (I hate bananas but love a banana milkshake—the curiosity got the better of me!) To begin, I broke down banana flesh using amylase enzymes, pectinase, and filtered water. Whilst I left this to sit, I infused Boatyard Vodka with the banana peel which would otherwise go to waste. I used Boatyard Vodka as the flavor from this is eerily reminiscent of bananas (and amazing).

After 48 hours, I filtered both end results and combined equal parts banana water and banana peel–infused Boatyard. I then added 50 milliliters (1²/₃ oz.) of lemon juice per liter of liquid (33.8 oz.). To this I added heated milk (approximately 200 milliliters or 7 oz.) and left it to sit for 24 hours—this was the clarification process. The addition of milk not only allows the drink to be clarified, but it also imparts creamy qualities that are present in milk, making for a wonderful drinking experience! After 24 hours, the milk will have curdled, and can then be filtered through coffee filters. This is one of the most time-consuming experiences I've endured—it has led me to purchasing additional filters and Kilner jars. Afterwards, I added gomme syrup to taste—it was delightful!

BELLE EPOQUE, NEW ORLEANS

Q & A WITH LAURA BELLUCCI, PROGRAM DIRECTOR

TELL US A BIT ABOUT HOW YOUR BAR GOT STARTED AND HOW YOU GOT INTO THE BUSINESS.

My bar is centered around telling the amazing history of the spirit of absinthe in Europe and New Orleans, as well as the history of our building, which dates back to 1806.

I have been bartending for 10 years. I started at a dive bar in Boston and then moved to New Orleans in 2013.

TELL US ABOUT THE GENERAL THEME OF YOUR BAR AND WHAT ROLE INFUSIONS PLAY IN YOUR COCKTAIL PROGRAM.

Belle Epoque looks to reference the era in France when absinthe rose to peak popularity. La Belle Époque was an era best characterized by the expression "joie de vivre," the exuberant enjoyment of life. This "beautiful era," lasted from the end of the Franco-Prussian War (1871) until the start of World War I (1914).

The decades prior were filled with revolution and terror, but during this time the standard of living improved for the people of France. There was growth in arts, entertainment, architecture, industry, and the culinary world, and an extreme sense of optimism for the future. We hope to provide an ambiance that echoes the joy and excitement of that era, while demystifying the story of absinthe and telling our building's incredible history. Belle Epoque will transport fated wanderers into the lamp-lit French cafés haunted by disheveled poets and the dizzy backrooms of illicit Prohibition-era dives.

We've developed an intoxicating tour, through the narrative of absinthe, that is both exotic and approachable. From classics like the Absinthe Frappe to a Herbsaint Apricot Zombie, we are sipping on the alchemy of the old and the new.

Executive chef Hayley Vanvleet creates delicious cuisine with a French accent, inspired by the creative spirit of the Belle Époque, and her menu aims to pair with absinthe and revelry. Join us on our adventure to untangle the sordid history of our patron saint, the captivating and damnable *la fée verte* ["the green fairy," a popular nickname for absinthe].

WHAT DO YOU LOOK FOR WHEN WORKING WITH OR CREATING INFUSIONS? HOW DO YOU USE THEM IN CREATING NEW COCKTAILS FOR YOUR MENU?

I look for elements that we already have in-house, and infusions that reduce waste (citrus peels, leftover bits from syrups, leftover herbs from the kitchen, etc.). I also look for whimsical flavors or something unexpected to the bar world—like breakfast cereal, candy, king cake—you name it. I draw most of my inspiration from the food world. I like things that are either premade and familiar, or exotic ingredients. For me it usually starts with a bizarre idea about a flavor and then I flesh it out around that. Sometimes ease of use is also a place I like to work from—in the sense that if something has a short shelf life or is difficult to breakdown and can be more easily showcased with an infusion—I will explore that.

DO YOU HAVE A FAVORITE SPIRIT TO WORK WITH WHEN MAKING YOUR INFUSIONS?

Gin is my favorite for herbs and robust flavors (grilled and smoked items). Absinthe blanche [clear absinthe] is my favorite for ripe fruit. Rum is my favorite for anything bread-, oat-, cake-, or cereal-related.

Many infusions require refrigeration to stay fresh. So having them on hand takes up precious fridge space. Also, if you have an extremely busy night and you run out, you can't immediately replace your mix. Infusions take time and love. I think it can also be difficult when an infusion goes awry, which is why little test batches are ideal.

I think bartenders are gaining enough experience with the infusion process that they are becoming able to make custom spirits that are exactly tailored to their menus and the flavor profiles that they are looking for. Tinctures are getting very popular and exciting, and are very much related to that strong desire to customize your products and make them particular to your bar. I think making more sustainable decisions, for example using infusions to reduce bar waste, is also gaining traction.

BAR BUONASERA, HONG KONG

Q & A WITH NICK TSE, BAR MANAGER

TELL US ABOUT THE GENERAL THEME OF YOUR BAR AND WHAT ROLE INFUSIONS PLAY IN YOUR COCKTAIL PROGRAM.

We call our theme *omakase*, which is similar to a chef's recommendation. We tailor-make the cocktails for the customer, based on their requests and feeling. We like to make the customer feel like it's their "own cocktail."

WHAT DO YOU LOOK FOR WHEN WORKING WITH AND CREATING INFUSIONS? HOW DO YOU USE THEM IN CREATING NEW COCKTAILS FOR YOUR MENU?

Most establishments use machines to speed up the process. We would like the customer to feel the flavors added by time, the ingredients infused in the spirits. By aging for few weeks to a few years and using a natural process instead of a mechanical process, we believe that the customer can feel the quality in something "hand-made."

DO YOU HAVE A FAVORITE SPIRIT TO WORK WITH WHEN MAKING YOUR INFUSIONS?

I prefer vodka, gin, and grappa. Those spirits make it easier to create different flavors and layers to enhance the original spirit.

WHAT IS THE HARDEST PART OF WORKING WITH INFUSIONS? ARE THERE ANY DOWNSIDES TO WORKING WITH INFUSION-BASED COCKTAILS?

The hardest part is getting the measurements right. Depending on the weather, we have to change the amounts for every ingredient to ensure the taste is what we want.

THE LEFT BANK BAR & RESTAURANT, YORK, PA

Q & A WITH MEGHAN ALLRED, BARTENDER

TELL US A BIT ABOUT YOURSELF AND HOW YOU GOT INTO THE BUSINESS.

In my earliest years my family traveled a lot due to my father being in the Navy. This gave me a love for travel and a respect for different cultures. As an adult I pursued a career in the entertainment field as a dancer and, eventually, an aerialist. I worked for a cruise line for seven years and this allowed me to continue to travel and learn about the many cultures outside of my home country. Once I decided to "hang up my heels," I needed to think about what came next. When deciding how to transition, I knew I needed a new career that mirrored my previous work. I wanted to be active and engaging. I love to think on my feet and knew my former training would help me excel at adapting to ever-changing surroundings and circumstances. I also wanted something that would challenge my creative side. My husband is a career bartender, and one with an exceptional flair. (Remember the movie *Cocktail*?) Seeing him at work reminded me of the fun and energetic atmosphere I loved about performing. Long story short, the decision was made, and I began a new path towards bartending.

TELL US ABOUT THE GENERAL THEME OF YOUR BAR AND WHAT ROLE INFUSIONS PLAY IN YOUR COCKTAIL PROGRAM.

We offer a casual yet sophisticated atmosphere with a menu that includes well thought out, seasonally inspired dishes as well as several longstanding favorites. Our cocktail list includes Signatures (guests favorites), Classics, Mocktails, and Seasonal options. We use infusions to enhance and/or complement the characteristics already present in our ingredients. Being new to the scene of bartending, infusions were one of the first techniques I felt comfortable playing with. Infusions are one of the easiest and, depending on the ingredients, frugal options for experimentation.

WHAT DO YOU LOOK FOR WHEN WORKING WITH OR CREATING INFUSIONS? HOW DO YOU USE THEM IN CREATING NEW COCKTAILS FOR YOUR MENU?

Have you ever really thought about infusions? They are everywhere! They can be as simple or as complicated as you make them. Think about that golden- or chocolatey-toned spirit at your local bar. It achieved that color by aging in a barrel of some sort. And, guess what? That is an infusion. The spirit slowly takes on the flavors, aroma, and color of the wood it rests in. Ever tried bitters in a cocktail? One of the oldest forms of infusion, it is the combination of ingredients such as spices, barks, roots, etc., with an overproof spirit. This combination slowly blends to form a highly concentrated product that seasons and adds that little something extra to your cocktail. And a little goes a long way! Have you ever added strawberries to your bubbly or cucumbers to your water? Those are also infusions. Infusions are all around!

When I am creating a beverage, flavor and aroma play an enormous role. Seasonality and sometimes a thematic approach can be utilized as well. Infusions are a wonderful way to complement a dish, further make use of an ingredient, or tease the taste buds. My personal process utilizes all of the above considerations. For example: I love working with florals in the spring, citrus and tropical elements in the summer, spices in the fall, and nuts or oils in the winter. But these guidelines are not exclusive and I keep an open mind which makes the possibilities limitless. After all, "one is only bound by the limits of one's imagination." When I create, I want my product to have layers of flavor and aroma. I want complexity even in simplicity, and I want to leave my guest thirsty for more!

DO YOU HAVE A FAVORITE SPIRIT TO WORK WITH WHEN MAKING YOUR INFUSIONS?

This one's easy: no. I love to keep an open mind, and admittedly there are spirits as well as ingredients that confuse me. Those are incredibly fun to work with as they are challenging, and they keep me from becoming complacent.

WHAT IS THE HARDEST PART OF WORKING WITH INFUSIONS? ARE THERE ANY DOWNSIDES TO WORKING WITH INFUSION-BASED COCKTAILS RELATIVE TO OTHER COCKTAILS?

Technique, timing, and temperature. Not all ingredients infuse in the same way or at the same rate. Some ingredients offer stages of flavors and you may not want all those flavors to become part of your infusion. Tea, for example, has lovely initial flavors ranging from floral, herbal, and fruity. It also contains very bitter and tannic characteristics that can leave a less desirable and lingering aftertaste. This can easily overshadow and ruin a beverage.

Regarding infusion-based cocktails, there are a number of downsides. First, the possible wait time. If you are not a patient person you could look at some of the quicker techniques available, such as working with a rapid infuser or sous vide. These tools will aid in speeding up the process; however, they have their own learning curve and the equipment will cost a bit depending on your budget. Second, let's talk about safety. While you can infuse with any number of ingredients, the safest way is to work with dehydrated products. Once the water content is extracted you avoid any risk of botulism, you increase the flavor by using more-concentrated ingredients, and you increase the shelf life of the infusion itself. Don't get me wrong, you can absolutely use fresh ingredients to make wonderful infusions. When you do, just make sure to store it well and enjoy it sooner rather than later.

CAN YOU TALK US THROUGH THE PROCESS YOU USE TO MAKE SOME OF YOUR INFUSIONS?

Aroma then flavor. Unless a theme is in play (say a holiday or special event), I begin with the aromas I detect in each ingredient or spirit. Then I take flavor into consideration, and this includes the obvious as well as the subtle. I really enjoy bringing out the subtle, more delicate flavors that make my guests go "Wow! I didn't taste that before."

IF INFUSIONS ARE JUST ONE PHASE IN THE DEVELOPMENT OF COCKTAILS, DO YOU HAVE ANY THOUGHTS ON WHAT COMES NEXT?

In the creative process I like to include all the senses. Infusions aid in the overall flavor and aroma, but I think you understand that by now. I also take into consideration the overall texture and presentation of the finished product. We eat (or, in this case, drink) with our eyes first. Aroma comes in second, followed by taste. Mouthfeel covers the sense of touch and further enhances a great beverage, whether it be light and bubbly, silky and smooth, or crisp and refreshing. And let's not forget sound. Yes, I have used pop rocks in a cocktail or two.

WHISKEY

MARIE LAVEAU

COURTESY OF SUGAR MONK

---

3 green
cardamom pods

3 drops of
orange bitters

1 black cardamom
pod

Applewood chips,
as needed

2 oz. Fliscouni-
Infused Bourbon

1 oz. Amaro
Averna

1. Place the cardamom pods in a mixing glass and muddle. Add all of the remaining ingredients, except for the applewood chips, fill the glass two-thirds of the way with ice, and stir until chilled.

2. Place the applewood chips in a smoking gun. Smoke the cocktail and then double-strain it into a coupe. Garnish with the torched strip of orange peel.

FLISCOUNI-INFUSED
BOURBON

1 (750 ml) bottle
of bourbon

2 bar spoons
fliscouni
(Greek watermint)

1. Place the fliscouni in the bourbon, seal, and let the mixture steep for 24 hours.

2. Double-strain before using or storing. For best results, use within 2 weeks.

TAMARILLO SUNSET

COURTESY OF HIDE BELOW

2 bar spoons fresh
lime juice

2½ oz. Tamarillo
& BJ Sauce

⅓ oz. Cocchi
Americano

1¼ oz. Starward
Two-Fold
Australian
Whiskey

2 bar spoons
Madeira

⅓ oz. Spiced
Honey Syrup

1. Place all of the ingredients in a cocktail shaker, fill it two-thirds of the way with ice, and shake until chilled.

2. Strain over ice into a highball glass and garnish with the dehydrated blood orange wheel and sprig of marjoram.

TAMARILLO & BJ SAUCE

4 tamarillo, peeled

3 cups cranberry juice

1 cup blood orange juice

1. Place the ingredients in a blender and puree until smooth.

2. Strain through cheesecloth before using or storing. This sauce will keep in the refrigerator for up to 2 weeks.

SPICED HONEY
SYRUP

1 cup water

1 cup honey

1 teaspoon grated
tonka bean

1 tablespoon
crushed pink
peppercorns

1. Place all of the ingredients in a vacuum bag. Seal and cook sous vide at 140°F for 30 minutes.

2. Strain before using or storing. This syrup will keep in the refrigerator for up to 1 month.

MICHTER'S & PEAR

COURTESY OF ARTESIAN

2 dashes of salt

1¼ oz. Pear
Cordial

1½ oz. Michter's
Bourbon

1. Place a large ice cube in a coupe.

2. Add the ingredients and stir until chilled.

PEAR
CORDIAL

2 oz. malic acid

3 lbs. pears, diced

1.8 oz. citric acid

1/3 oz. vodka

15 cups water

9¼ cups sugar

1. Place all of the ingredients, except for the vodka, in a vacuum bag and seal it. Refrigerate for 24 hours.

2. Strain the cordial through coffee filters or cheesecloth and stir in the vodka. The cordial will keep in the refrigerator for up to 1 month.

> **NOTE:** Artesian uses Passe Crassane pears when making this cordial.

THE NEW YORK
HIGHBALL

COURTESY OF TRAVEL BAR

2 oz. Mint-Infused
Bourbon

2 dashes of
Scrappy's
Chocolate Bitters

Seltzer water,
to top

1. Place the bourbon and bitters in a mixing glass, fill it two-thirds of the way with ice, and stir until chilled.

2. Strain over ice into a Collins glass, top with the seltzer, and garnish with the sprig of mint.

MINT-INFUSED
BOURBON

1½ cups fresh
spearmint

1 (1.75 l) bottle
of Eagle Rare
Bourbon

1. Place the ingredients in a large mason jar and store in a cool, dry place for 5 days, agitating the mixture occasionally.

2. Double-strain before using or storing. For best results, use the infusion within 2 weeks.

SPICY BOURBON

COURTESY OF DIAMOND DOGS

3 star anise, crushed

4 cups bourbon

3 cinnamon sticks

8 whole cloves

10 allspice berries

2 peppercorns

1. Place the cinnamon sticks in a dry skillet and toast over medium heat until browned. Place the cinnamon sticks in a large mason jar and add the remaining spices to the pan. Toast, shaking the pan frequently, until they start to smoke. Add them to the mason jar and pour the bourbon over the top.

2. Let the mixture steep for 4 to 7 days, until the flavor is to your liking. For best results, use within 2 weeks.

NOTE: To bolster the flavor of this bourbon, add 1½ cups of Barrow's Intense Ginger Liqueur to the mason jar before steeping.

ELEVATED
BRILLIANCE

COURTESY OF MEGHANN ALLRED

GARNISH: 3 RECYCLED ESPRESSO BEANS

1½ oz. Paul John
Brilliance whiskey

½ oz. Cardamom
Honey Syrup

¼ oz. fresh
lemon juice

¼ oz. Toasted
Cocoa Nib &
Espresso Brew

1. Place a coupe in the freezer.

2. Place all of the ingredients in a cocktail shaker, fill it two-thirds of
    the way with ice, and shake until chilled.

3. Strain into the chilled coupe and garnish with the Recycled
    Espresso Beans.

CARDAMOM
HONEY SYRUP

½ cup wildflower
honey

¼ cup water

½ teaspoon
ground cardamom

1. Place all of the ingredients in a saucepan and simmer over medium-low heat until the honey has emulsified. Remove from heat and let cool.

2. Strain the syrup through fine mesh before using or storing. The syrup will keep in the refrigerator for up to 1 month.

RECYCLED ESPRESSO
BEANS

1 chocolate bar
(60 percent
cocoa preferred),
melted

½ tablespoon
reserved cocoa
nib & espresso
solids

1. Place the ingredients in a mixing bowl and stir to combine.

2. Pour the mixture into a silicone coffee bean mold. If this mold is not available, the mixture can also be spread on a parchment-lined baking sheet to make a kind of bark.

3. Place in freezer until set, about 10 minutes. Remove the beans from the mold and use as desired. Store any leftover beans in the refrigerator, where they will keep for up to 1 month.

TOASTED COCOA NIB
& ESPRESSO BREW

½ teaspoon cocoa
nibs, ground

1 oz. lukewarm
water (90°F)

½ teaspoon finely
ground espresso

1. Place the cocoa nibs in a dry skillet and toast over medium heat, shaking the pan frequently, until they start to sweat and become extremely fragrant, about 10 minutes.

2. Place the cocoa nibs in a mason jar, add the remaining ingredients, and cover the jar. Let steep at room temperature for at least 4 hours, though steeping overnight will produce better results.

3. Strain the mixture through fine mesh before using or storing. Reserve the solids for use in the Recycled Espresso Beans. The brew will keep inthe refrigerator for up to 1 week.

LORD FANNY

COURTESY OF DIAMOND DOGS

2 dashes of
Angostura Bitters

1 oz. Amaro
Averna

2 oz. Rooibos–
Infused Monkey
Shoulder

1. Chill a coupe in the freezer.

2. Place all of the ingredients in a mixing glass, fill it two-thirds of the way with ice, and stir until chilled.

3. Strain into the chilled coupe and garnish with the strip of lemon peel.

ROOIBOS-INFUSED MONKEY SHOULDER

3 bags of
rooibos tea

1 (750 ml) bottle
of Monkey
Shoulder Blended
Scotch Whisky

1. Place the ingredients in a mason jar and steep for 24 hours.

2. Remove the tea bags and use as desired. For best results, use within 2 weeks.

FEELING SINGLE,
SEEING DOUBLE

COURTESY OF TRAVEL BAR

---

2 oz. Cherry–
Infused Rye

1. Place the rye in a cocktail shaker, fill it two-thirds of the way with ice, and shake until chilled.

2. Use a Hawthorne strainer to strain the cocktail into a coupe. Run a bamboo pick through the Cherry Ice Cube and rest it on the glass.

CHERRY ICE CUBES: Place 3 dried cherries in each well in an ice cube tray. Add ¼ oz. Rothman & Winter Orchard Cherry liqueur to each well, and then top with water. Cover the tray with plastic wrap and freeze until solid.

CHERRY-INFUSED
RYE

2 (750 ml) bottles
of rye whiskey

½ lb. dried
cherries

1. Place the rye and cherries in a large mason jar and store in a cool, dry place for 11 days, agitating the mixture occasionally.

2. Strain before using or storing. For best results, use within 2 weeks.

TO CY
& LEE

COURTESY OF HUMBERTO FLORES

½ oz. Calendula
& Cedar Syrup

2 oz. Calendula
& Chrysanthemum
Bourbon

1. Place all of the ingredients in a cocktail shaker, fill it two-thirds of the way with ice, and shake until chilled.

2. Strain over ice into an Old Fashioned glass.

A bartender by trade, Humberto Flores is one of those uncommonly generous masters who seem to have an endless supply of tricks up their sleeves, and no problem sharing them with an enthusiastic novice. That combination made him a natural for this project.

½ oz. sweet
vermouth

½ oz. dry
vermouth

1 teaspoon
Calvados

CALENDULA &CHRYSANTHEMUM
BOURBON

1 (750 ml) bottle
of bourbon

1 oz. calendula
blossoms

1 oz.
chrysanthemum
blossoms

1. Place all of the ingredients in a large mason jar and steep in a cool, dark place for 48 hours.

2. Strain before using or storing. For best results, use within 2 weeks.

CALENDULA & CEDAR
SYRUP

35 oz. boiling
water

0.15 oz. calendula
blossoms

0.2 oz. cedar
wood shavings*

20 oz. sugar

1. Pour the boiling water over the calendula blossoms and cedar shavings. Let the mixture steep at room temperature for 24 hours.

2. Strain into a saucepan, add the sugar, and cook over medium heat until the mixture has reduced, stirring constantly to dissolve the sugar. Remove from heat and let cool before using or storing. The syrup will keep in the refrigerator for up to 1 month.

NOTE: Carboxylic acid naturally occurs in cedar and may provoke allergic reactions.

INDIAN SUMMER

COURTESY OF HUMBERTO FLORES

¼ oz. honey syrup

¼ oz fresh lemon juice

¾ oz. Amaro Averna

2 dashes of orange bitters

¼ oz. Bénédictine

2 oz. Walnut, Pecan & Almond Whiskey

¼ oz. fresh orange juice

1. Place all of the ingredients in a cocktail shaker, fill it two-thirds of the way with ice, and shake until chilled.

2. Strain into a coupe.

WALNUT, PECAN & ALMOND WHISKEY

2 oz. pecans, crushed

1 oz. walnuts, crushed

1 oz. almonds, shaved

20 oz. preferred whiskey

1. Place all of the ingredients in a mason jar and let the mixture steep in a cool, dark place for 48 hours.

2. Strain before using or storing. For best results, use within 2 weeks.

PINE TREE

COURTESY OF HUMBERTO FLORES

2 oz. Pine & Tamarind Bourbon

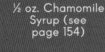

½ oz. Chamomile Syrup (see page 154)

½ oz. tamarind liqueur

½ oz. fresh lime juice

½ oz. Luxardo maraschino liqueur

1. Place all of the ingredients in a cocktail shaker, fill it two-thirds of the way with ice, and shake until chilled.

2. Strain over ice into an Old Fashioned glass.

PINE & TAMARIND
BOURBON

3 oz. pine needles

10 oz. boiling water

5 oz. tamarind pulp

1 (750 ml) bottle of whiskey

1. Place the pine needles and boiling water in a container and let the mixture steep for 24 hours.

2. Strain the water and add the tamarind pulp. Let the mixture steep for 24 hours.

3. Place the mixture in a blender and puree until smooth. Strain, place the liquid in a large mason jar, and add the whiskey. Let the mixture steep for at least 24 hours.

4. Strain before using or storing. For best results, use within 2 weeks.

GRILLED SATSUMA
LOUISIANNE

COURTESY OF LAURA BELLUCCI/BELLE EPOQUE

GARNISH: 1 STRIP OF ORANGE PEEL

2 tablespoons honey

4 oz. Peychaud's Bitters

1 (750 ml) bottle of La Quintineye Vermouth Royal Rouge

1 pinch of cinnamon

1 (750 ml) bottle of Sazerac Rye

1 teaspoon coconut oil

1 (750 ml) bottle of Bénédictine

10 to 12 satsuma oranges, halved

4 oz. Herbsaint or absinthe

1. Preheat your gas or charcoal grill to 450°F. Place the honey, cinnamon, and coconut oil in a small bowl and stir to combine. Brush the mixture on the cut sides of the oranges.

2. Place the oranges on the grill, cut side down, and grill until marks appear, 3 to 5 minutes. Remove from the grill and let cool.

3. When the oranges have cooled, place them in an airtight container. Place the remaining ingredients in a bowl and stir to combine. Pour the mixture over the oranges, cover the container, and refrigerate for 48 hours.

4. Strain before using and serve over ice, garnishing each drink with a strip of orange peel.

VODKA

THE
NORDIC

COURTESY OF TRAVEL BAR

2 oz. Lemon & Dill
Vodka

1 oz. fresh-
pressed cucumber
juice

1. Place the ingredients in a cocktail shaker, fill it two-thirds of the way with ice, and shake until chilled.

2. Use a julep strainer to strain the cocktail into a coupe and garnish with the lemon twist.

LEMON &
DILL VODKA

2 (750 ml)
bottles of vodka
(Wheatley
preferred)

2 bunches of fresh
dill, bottom parts
of stems removed

2 lemon rinds

1. Place all of the ingredients in a large mason jar and store in a cool, dry place for 13 days, agitating the mixture occasionally.

2. Double-strain before using or storing. For best results, use within 2 weeks.

B.L.P.D.

COURTESY OF BABEL

1. Add all of the ingredients to a cocktail shaker, fill it two-thirds of the way with ice, and shake until chilled.

2. Double-strain into a coupe and add an ice cube if desired. Garnish with the basil leaves and cracked black pepper.

½ oz. fresh
lime juice

¾ oz. Strawberry
& Pepper Shrub

½ oz. Basil &
Honey Syrup

1½ oz. Belvedere
Pink Grapefruit
vodka

BASIL & HONEY
SYRUP

2 cups honey

1 cup water

Leaves from 5 sprigs of fresh basil

1. Place all of the ingredients in a vacuum bag and seal it.

2. Sous vide for 4 to 5 hours at 140°F. Strain through cheesecloth before using or storing. This syrup will keep in the refrigerator for up to 1 month.

STRAWBERRY &
PEPPER SHRUB

½ lb. strawberries,
hulled and sliced

4 oz. sugar

2 teaspoons
coarsely ground
black pepper

1 cup apple cider
vinegar

1. Place the strawberries, sugar, and pepper in a large jar, seal, and shake to combine. Store in the refrigerator for at least 2 hours and up to 1 day.

2. Add the vinegar, seal, shake to combine, and store in the refrigerator for 2 days

3. Strain the mixture through a fine sieve, transfer the liquid to a mason jar, and shake to incorporate any undissolved sugar. Transfer to the refrigerator and let stand for 1 week before using. The shrub will keep in the refrigerator for up to 2 months.

BLOODY
MARTINI

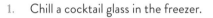

1¼ oz. Ancho-Infused Vodka

¾ oz. Noilly Prat Dry Vermouth

2 teaspoons Vin Jaune

1²/₃ oz. Consomme

1. Chill a cocktail glass in the freezer.

2. Place all of the ingredients in a mixing glass, fill it two-thirds of the way with ice, and stir until chilled.

3. Strain into the chilled cocktail glass.

CONSOMME

15 tomatoes

¾ oz. smoked
paprika

½ oz. chopped
fresh herbs

Salt and pepper,
to taste

1. Cut the tomatoes into quarters. Working in batches, place them in a food processor. Pulse until minced and transfer them to a saucepan.

2. Bring the tomatoes to a boil over medium-high heat. While the tomatoes are warming, line a fine sieve with a coffee filter and place the paprika and fresh herbs in it.

3. When the tomatoes start to boil, ladle them into the coffee filter and sprinkle each addition with salt and pepper. Press down to extract as much liquid from the tomatoes as possible. Transfer the strained liquid to a vacuum bag and seal it. Refrigerate for 3 days before using. This will keep in the refrigerator for up to 1 week once ready to use.

ANCHO-INFUSED
VODKA

1. Place the ingredients in a large mason jar and steep for 30 minutes.

2. Strain before using or storing. For best results, use within 2 weeks.

2 dried ancho chili peppers

1 (750 ml) bottle of Grey Goose Vodka

BUNNY
ARABICUM

COURTESY OF RABBITHOLE

1/3 oz. freshly brewed espresso

1½ oz. Cardamom-Infused Vodka

2/3 oz. simple syrup

2/3 oz. Cointreau

1/3 oz. Monin Turmeric Syrup

1. Place all of the ingredients in a cocktail shaker, fill it two-thirds of the way with ice, and shake until chilled.

2. Strain into a coupe and garnish with the sprig of mint.

CARDAMOM-INFUSED
VODKA

5 cardamom
pods, crushed

1 (750 ml) bottle
of vodka

1. Add the cardamom pods to the bottle of vodka and let the mixture steep at room temperature for 48 hours.

2. Strain before using or storing. For best results, use within 2 weeks.

MOSCOW MULE

COURTESY OF NICK TSE/BAR BUONASERA

1 oz. Ginger-Infused Vodka

½ oz. Seifuku Awamori ginger liqueur

⅓ oz. fresh lime juice

Asahi Wilkinson Ginger Ale, to top

1. Add the vodka, ginger liqueur, and lime juice to a copper mule mug filled with ice and stir.

2. Top with the ginger ale and garnish with the lime wheel.

GINGER-INFUSED
VODKA

¼ cup thinly
sliced ginger

1 (750 ml)
bottle of vodka

1. Place the sliced ginger in the bottle of vodka and let it steep for 2 weeks.

2. Strain before using or storing. For best results, use within 2 weeks.

WIDOW'S BLOODY MARY

COURTESY OF NICK TSE/BAR BUONASERA

3 dashes of
Worcestershire
sauce

5 dashes of
Tabasco Green
Pepper Sauce

1¹/₃ oz. Spicy
Vodka

Dash of black
pepper

¹/₃ bar spoon
celery salt

1¹/₃ oz. Clamato

1 slice of tomato
(Bar Buonasera
uses Japanese
Black Trifele
tomatoes)

1. Add all of the ingredients to a cocktail shaker, fill it two-thirds of the way with ice, and shake until chilled.

2. Strain over ice into a double Old Fashioned glass and garnish with the lemon wheel.

SPICY VODKA

1 (750 ml) bottle of vodka

1 Japanese tomato, sliced

1 celery stalk, chopped

1 teaspoon green peppercorns

1 green chili pepper, sliced

1 teaspoon black peppercorns

1 red chili pepper, sliced

6 fresh basil leaves

1. Place all of the ingredients in a large mason jar and let the mixture steep in a cool, dark place for about 2 weeks.

2. Strain before using or storing. For best results, use within 2 weeks.

HOUSE OF
THE RIND

COURTESY OF LAURA BELLUCCI/BELLE EPOQUE

2 drops of 18.21
Chamomile Bitters

1 oz. lemon curd

¾ oz. fresh lemon
juice

1½ oz. Earl Grey–
Intused Cathead
Honeysuckle
Vodka

1. Place all of the ingredients in a cocktail shaker, fill it two-thirds of the way with ice, and shake until chilled.

2. Double-strain into a coupe. Express the lemon peel over the cocktail and then use it as a garnish alongside the butter cookie.

ACCORDING TO LAURA BELLUCCI, "Tea infusions are probably my favorite in the world. They are quick to make and there are endless combinations to enjoy. This cocktail is my very best attempt to showcase the beautiful flavors of Earl Grey tea and lemon in a playful way."

EARL GREY-INFUSED
VODKA

3 bags of Earl
Grey tea

1 (750 ml) bottle
of Cathead
Honeysuckle
Vodka

1. Place the tea bags and vodka in a large mason jar and steep for 4 hours.

2. Remove the tea bags and strain before using or storing. For best results, use within 2 weeks.

YEAR OF THE CAT

COURTESY OF HUMBERTO FLORES

¼ oz. simple syrup

2½ oz. Lemon Balm & Verbena Vodka

¾ oz. Lillet Blanc

1 teaspoon absinthe

½ oz. pineapple juice

1. Place all of the ingredients in a cocktail shaker, fill it two-thirds of the way with ice, and shake until chilled.

2. Strain into a coupe.

LEMON BALM &
VERBENA VODKA

0.1 oz. dried
lemon balm

0.1 oz. dried
verbena

20 oz. vodka

1. Place the ingredients in a mason jar and let the mixture steep for 48 hours.

2. Strain before using or storing. For best results, use within 2 weeks.

TRAS TUS OJOS

COURTESY OF HUMBERTO FLORES

2 oz. Camellia & Peach Vodka

1 oz. fresh lemon juice

½ oz. St-Germain

½ oz. Suze

2 dashes of peach bitters

1. Place all of the ingredients in a cocktail shaker, fill it two-thirds of the way with ice, and shake until chilled.

2. Strain into a coupe.

CAMELLIA & PEACH
VODKA

0.1 oz. camellia leaves

3 bags of peach tea

20 oz. vodka

1. Place the ingredients in a mason jar and let the mixture steep for 48 hours.

2. Strain before using or storing. For best results, use within 2 weeks.

THYME FOR HARVEY

COURTESY OF HUMBERTO FLORES

2 oz. Celery
Seed Vodka

½ oz. Orange
& Thyme Syrup

½ oz. Galliano

1 oz. orange juice

2 dashes of
grapefruit bitters

1. Place all of the ingredients in a cocktail shaker, fill it two-thirds of the way with ice, and shake until chilled.

2. Strain over ice into a highball glass and garnish with a slice of orange.

CELERY SEED
VODKA

1. Place the ingredients in a mason jar and let the mixture steep for 48 hours.

2. Strain before using or storing. For best results, use within 2 weeks.

0.3 oz. celery seeds

20 oz. vodka

ORANGE & THYME
SYRUP

1. Place the orange peel, thyme, and boiling water in a large mason jar and let the mixture steep until cool.

2. Strain, transfer to a saucepan, and add the sugar. Bring to a boil over medium heat and cook until reduced by half, stirring to dissolve the sugar. Let cool before using or storing. This syrup will keep in the refrigerator for up to 1 month.

1 orange peel

0.1 oz. dried thyme

20 oz. boiling water

10 oz. sugar

GIN

GIN & CASSIS
HIGHBALL
COURTESY OF ARTESIAN

Dash of salt

1 oz. Cassis
Leaf Cordial

1²/₃ oz. Oxley Gin

2 oz. club soda

1. Place the salt, cordial, and gin in a mixing glass, fill it two-thirds of the way with ice, and stir until chilled.

2. Pour the club soda into a highball glass with ice and strain the cocktail into the glass.

CASSIS LEAF
CORDIAL

15 cups water

2.1 oz. dried
cassis leaves

5 lbs. sugar

1/3 oz. vodka

4½ oz. citric acid

1.4 oz. lactic acid

1. Place all of the ingredients, except for the vodka, in a large container and let the mixture steep for 48 hours.

2. Strain through a coffee filter, stir in the vodka, and use as desired. The cordial will keep in the refrigerator for up to 1 month.

THE
3151

COURTESY OF TRAVEL BAR

GARNISH: 1 ORANGE TWIST & 1 INFUSED FIG

2½ oz. Fig-Infused
Gin

½ oz. Nux Alpina
Walnut Liqueur

2 dashes of
Bittercube Bolivar
Bitters

1. Place the ingredients in a mixing glass, fill it two-thirds of the way with ice, and stir until chilled.

2. Strain into a double Old Fashioned glass containing one large ice cube and garnish with the orange twist and infused fig.

FIG-INFUSED
GIN

18 dried Turkish
figs, halved

2 (750 ml) bottles
of Aria Portland
Dry Gin

1. Place the ingredients in a large mason jar and store in a cool, dry place for 2 weeks, agitating the mixture occasionally.

2. Strain before using or storing. Reserve the infused figs for garnish. For best results, use within 2 weeks.

HIBALL
SO HARD

COURTESY OF ZACHARY SHARAGA & RAMI LEVY

GARNISH: 1 TO 2 BAY LEAVES, 1 MEYER LEMON TWIST & 3 COFFEE BEANS

2 oz. Coffee-
Infused Gin

4 oz. Q Tonic
Water

1 dash of lactic
acid (optional)

1. Chill a highball glass in the freezer.

2. Fill the glass with ice and build the cocktail in the glass, stirring gently to combine.

3. Garnish with 1 or 2 bay leaves, the Meyer lemon twist, and the coffee beans.

This cocktail comes via Dear Mama Manhattanville, the latest project from spirits industry veteran Zachary Sharaga. They focus on all things coffee, and have been so readily embraced that they just opened up a second location. Zachary has just two suggestions for the home infuser: "Label!" and store your infusions in the refrigerator.

COFFEE-INFUSED
GIN

1 (750 ml) bottle
of London Dry gin

4½ oz. medium–
roast coffee
beans

1. Add the ingredients to a mason jar and let steep for 3 to 4 hours, agitating the mixture halfway through.

2. Strain before using or storing. For best results, use within 2 weeks.

NO SUCH
THING

COURTESY OF COUPETTE

¾ oz. Bombay
Sapphire Gin

½ oz. Rhubarb
Cordial

1 oz. Lillet Rose

1 bar spoon Zucca
Rabarbaro liqueur

⅓ oz. Suze

⅓ oz. Campari

1. Place all of the ingredients in a mixing glass, fill it two-thirds of the way with ice, and stir until chilled.

2. Strain into a Nick & Nora glass containing an ice sphere.

RHUBARB
CORDIAL

½ lb. rhubarb, trimmed and chopped

1 cup caster sugar

1 cup water

1 teaspoon 5% Citric Acid Solution

1. Place the rhubarb, sugar, and water in a vacuum bag, seal it, and cook it sous vide at 149°F for 1 hour.

2. Strain, stir in the 5% Citric Acid Solution, and use as desired. The cordial will keep in the refrigerator for up to 2 months.

5% CITRIC ACID SOLUTION: Dissolve 2 teaspoons of citric acid in 2 cups of boiling water and use as desired.

ROSEMARY
MARTINI

COURTESY OF NICK TSE/BAR BUONASERA

GARNISH: 1 OLIVE & 1 LEMON TWIST

½ oz. Rosemary
& Pepper Grappa

4 oz. Tanqueray
Gin

⅓ oz. Noilly Prat
Dry Vermouth

1. Place all of the ingredients in a mixing glass, fill it two-thirds of the way with ice, and stir until chilled.

2. Strain into a cocktail glass and garnish with the olive and the lemon twist.

ROSEMARY & PEPPER
GRAPPA

1 tablespoon black peppercorns

4 sprigs of fresh rosemary

1 (500 ml) bottle of La Valdotaine Grappa

1. Place all of the ingredients in a large mason jar and let steep in a cool, dark place for 2 weeks.

2. Strain before using or storing. For best results, use within 2 weeks.

ROYAL RABBIT

COURTESY OF RABBITHOLE

GARNISH: 1 STRIP OF LEMON PEEL

2/3 oz. Lavender-
Infused Gin

2 oz. Champagne,
to top

2/3 oz. gin

2/3 oz. fresh lemon
juice

2/3 oz. simple
syrup

1. Add all of the ingredients, except for the Champagne, to a cocktail shaker, fill it two-thirds of the way with ice, and shake until chilled.

2. Strain into a coupe, top with the Champagne, and garnish with the strip of lemon peel.

LAVENDER-INFUSED
GIN

1 (750 ml) bottle
of gin

4 sprigs of fresh
lavender

1. Place all of the ingredients in a large mason jar and let steep at room temperature for 48 hours.

2. Strain before using or storing. For best results, use within 2 weeks.

BUNNY ON THE BEACH

COURTESY OF RABBITHOLE

Club soda, to top

1 oz. Blood
Orange Syrup

1 oz. fresh lemon
juice

1½ oz.
Cardamom–
Infused Gin

1. Add the ingredients to a highball glass filled with ice in the order they are listed and stir until chilled. Garnish with the dehydrated blood orange wheel.

CARDAMOM-INFUSED
GIN

1 (750 ml) bottle
of gin

5 cardamom
pods, crushed

1. Place all of the ingredients in a large mason jar and let steep at room temperature for 48 hours.

2. Strain before using or storing. For best results, use within 2 weeks.

BLOOD ORANGE
SYRUP

1 cup sugar

1 cup fresh blood orange juice

1. Place all of the ingredients in a saucepan and simmer over medium heat, stirring until the sugar has dissolved.

2. Remove the pan from heat and let cool before using or storing. This syrup will keep in the refrigerator for up to 1 month.

STATEN MAN
MARTINI

COURTESY OF LAURA BELLUCCI/BELLE EPOQUE

GARNISH: 1 STRIP OF GRAPEFRUIT PEEL WRAPPED AROUND CAPERS

1½ oz. Grilled Artichoke Gin

½ oz. Cynar

½ oz. Dolin Blanc vermouth

2 drops of El Guapo Crawfish Boil Bitters

1. Place the ingredients in a mixing glass, fill it two-thirds of the way with ice, and stir until chilled.

2. Strain into a coupe and garnish with the capers wrapped in a grapefruit peel.

GRILLED ARTICHOKE
GIN

8 artichokes,
halved

Olive oil, as
needed

1 (750 ml) bottle
of Gentilly Gin

1. Preheat your gas or charcoal grill to 450°F. Lightly coat the cut sides of the artichokes with olive oil, place them on the grill, cut side down, and grill until they start to char, 3 to 5 minutes.

2. Place the grilled artichokes and the gin in a mason jar, cover, and store in the refrigerator for 3 to 4 days. Strain before using or storing. For best results, use within 2 weeks.

THE FRENCH CHEF

COURTESY OF LAURA BELLUCCI/BELLE EPOQUE

1 drop of
Angostura Bitters

1 drop of
The Bitter Truth
Lemon Bitters

1 oz. Noilly Prat
Ambré

½ oz. Noilly Prat
Extra Dry

2 oz. Grilled
Peach & Tarragon
Gin

1. Place the ingredients in a mixing glass, fill it two-thirds of the way with ice, and stir until chilled.

2. Strain into a coupe containing one ice cube.

GRILLED PEACH &
TARRAGON GIN

4 peaches, halved
and pitted

2 handfuls of
fresh tarragon
leaves

1 (750 ml) bottle
of Plymouth Gin

1. Preheat your gas or charcoal grill to 450°F. Place the peaches on the grill, cut side down, and grill until they start to char, 3 to 5 minutes.

2. Place the peaches, tarragon leaves, and gin in a large mason jar and let steep in a cool place for 24 to 48 hours.

3. Strain before using or storing. For best results, use within 2 weeks.

LAURA BELLUCCI: "This was my very first foray into grilled infusions, and it provides a relatively big wow for very little effort."

ROOF GARDEN SIPPER

COURTESY OF BABEL

GARNISH: 1 STRIP OF LEMON PEEL & 1 SPRIG OF FRESH ROSEMARY

1 oz. Hendrick's Gin

¼ oz. Chamomile Syrup

½ oz. St-Germain

2 dashes of lemon bitters

²/₃ oz. fresh lemon juice

2 dashes of rose water

¼ oz. rose syrup

1 egg white

1. Chill a coupe in the freezer.

2. Add all of the ingredients to a cocktail shaker and dry shake for 15 seconds. Add ice and shake until chilled.

3. Double-strain into the chilled coupe and garnish with the strip of lemon peel and the sprig of rosemary.

CHAMOMILE
SYRUP

2 cups water

2 cups sugar

3 tablespoons
loose-leaf
chamomile tea

1. Place the water and sugar in a saucepan and bring to a boil, stirring until the sugar has dissolved.

2. Remove the saucepan from heat, add the chamomile tea, and let steep until the mixture has cooled completely.

3. Strain before using or storing. This syrup will keep in the refrigerator for up to 1 month.

TEATIME ACROSS THE POND

COURTESY OF MEGHANN ALLRED

GARNISH: 1 SPRIG OF FRESH MINT & ICED SCOTCH SHORTBREAD

2½ oz. Green
Tea–Infused Gin

½ oz. Raspberry
Syrup

¼ oz. Yellow
Chartreuse

1. Chill a teacup or coupe in the freezer.

2. Place all of the all ingredients in a cocktail shaker, fill it two-thirds of the way with ice, and shake until chilled.

3. Strain into the chilled cup and garnish with a sprig of mint and Iced Scotch Shortbread.

GREEN TEA-INFUSED
GIN

½ cup Aviation
Gin

1 bag or 1
teaspoon loose-
leaf organic green
tea

1. Place the gin and tea in a mason jar and let it steep at room temperature until the flavor is bright, about 25 minutes.

2. Strain before using or storing. For best results, use within 2 weeks.

RASPBERRY SYRUP

7 large
raspberries

½ cup sugar

½ cup water

1. Place the raspberries in a saucepan and muddle. Add the sugar and water, stir to combine, and simmer over medium heat, stirring to dissolve the sugar.

2. Remove from heat and let cool. Strain before using or storing. This syrup will keep in the refrigerator for up to 1 month.

ICED SCOTCH
SHORTBREAD

2½ sticks of
unsalted butter

Easy Icing, as
needed

½ cup sugar, plus
2 tablespoons

Rainbow sprinkles,
for topping

2½ cups all-
purpose flour

1 teaspoon kosher
salt

1. Preheat the oven to 325°F. Grate the butter into a bowl and place it in the freezer for 30 minutes.

2. Place the ½ cup of sugar, flour, salt, and frozen butter in the work bowl of a stand mixer and beat slowly until it is fine like sand. Be careful not to overwork the mixture.

3. Press the mixture into a square 8-inch baking pan and bake for 1 hour and 15 minutes.

4. Remove from oven and sprinkle the remaining sugar over the top. Let cool, spread the icing over the shortbread, and distribute the rainbow sprinkles over the top. Let the icing set and then cut the shortbread into bars.

> **EASY ICING:** Place 1 cup confectioners' sugar, 1 tablespoon hot water (125°F), and 1 teaspoon Green Tea–Infused Gin in a mixing bowl and stir until the icing has the desired consistency.

AFTERNOON
TEA

COURTESY OF MEGHANN ALLRED

GARNISH: 2 RASPBERRIES & 1 SPRIG OF FRESH MINT

1½ oz. Green Tea–
Infused Gin (see
page 158)

½ oz. Raspberry
Syrup (see
page 159)

Soda water, to top

1. Place the gin and syrup in a highball glass with ice and stir to combine.

2. Top with the soda water and garnish with the raspberries and sprig of mint.

NOTE: If raspberries are out of season, substitute the Chamomile Syrup on page 154 for the Raspberry Syrup.

BEETROOT

COURTESY OF ARTESIAN

1¼ oz. Star of
Bombay Gin

½ oz. Beetroot
Distillate

1¼ oz. Raw
Beetroot Cordial

½ oz. Cooked
Beetroot Cordial

1. Pour the ingredients into a wine glass and stir to combine.

NOTE: To make a batch version of this cocktail, combine 23²/₃ oz. Star of Bombay Gin, 10 oz. Beetroot Distillate, 23²/₃ oz. Raw Beetroot Cordial, 10 oz. Cooked Beetroot Cordial, and 47 oz. water.

BEETROOT
DISTILLATE

Salt, as needed

2½ lbs. golden beets

80 oz. vodka

1. Preheat the oven to 350°F. Cover a baking sheet with a bed of salt, place the beets on top of the salt, and roast in the oven for 2 hours. Remove from the oven and let the beets cool.

2. Peel the beets and place them in a centrifuge with the vodka. Process for 30 minutes at 14°F.

3. Place the liquid in a rotavap and distill at 35 mbar. Distill until you have about 50 oz., about 1½ hours. For best results, use within 2 weeks.

RAW BEETROOT CORDIAL

67²/₃ oz. water

1²/₃ oz. malic acid

1. Place all of the ingredients in a vacuum bag, seal, and refrigerate for 2 hours.

2. Strain before using or storing. The cordial will keep in the refrigerator for up to 2 months.

3½ oz. vodka

1/₃ oz. tartaric acid

4¼ lbs. sugar

1 teaspoon citric acid

2¼ lbs. golden beets, peeled and diced

½ teaspoon ascorbic acid

COOKED BEETROOT
CORDIAL

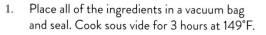

67²/₃ oz. water   ¹/₃ oz. tartaric acid

1²/₃ oz. malic acid   1 teaspoon citric acid

2½ lbs. sugar   Pinch of ascorbic acid

4½ lbs. golden beets, peeled and diced

1. Place all of the ingredients in a vacuum bag and seal. Cook sous vide for 3 hours at 149°F.

2. Strain before using or storing. The cordial will last in the refrigerator for up to 2 months.

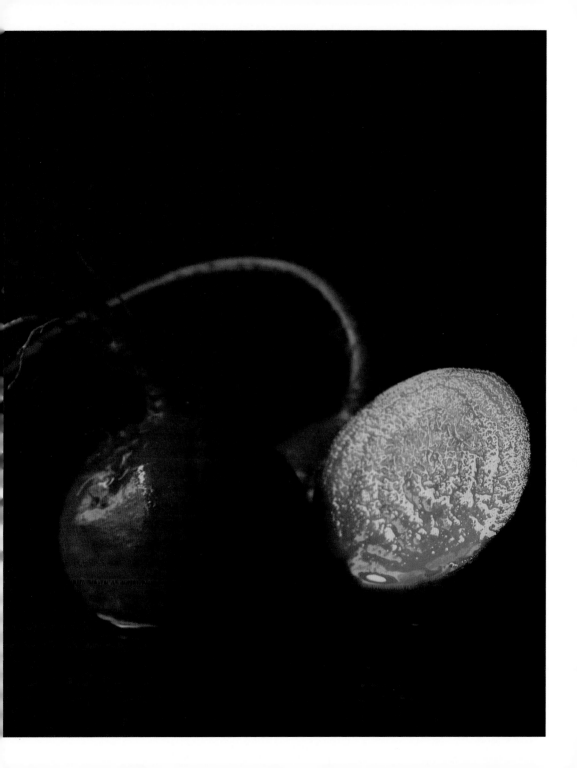

SILK STOCKING

COURTESY OF BREA FREDERICK & BEAU GAULTIER

GARNISH: 1 DRIED ROSEBUD

1½ oz. Lavender-Infused Boodles Gin

2 oz. Banfi Rosa Regale, to top

¾ oz. fresh lemon juice

¼ oz. simple syrup

½ oz. Marie Brizard Parfait Amour

1. Place all of the ingredients, except for the sparkling wine, in a cocktail shaker, fill it two-thirds of the way with ice, and shake until chilled.

2. Strain into a champagne flute, top with the sparkling wine, and garnish with the dried rosebud.

LAVENDER-INFUSED
BOODLES GIN

1 (750 ml) bottle
of Boodles Gin

4 sprigs of fresh
lavender

1. Place the ingredients in a mason jar and let steep at room temperature for 48 hours.

2. Strain before using or storing. For best results, use within 2 weeks.

BEAUTIFUL PEA
GREEN BOAT

COURTESY OF HUMBERTO FLORES

2 oz. Lemongrass
& Coriander Gin

3 oz. Prosecco

½ oz. Green
Chartreuse

½ oz. fresh lime
juice

¾ oz. Lemongrass
Syrup (see
page 278)

1. Place all of the ingredients, except for the Prosecco, in a cocktail shaker, fill it two-thirds of the way with ice, and shake until chilled.

2. Strain into a coupe or a champagne flute, top with the Prosecco, and serve.

LEMONGRASS &
CORIANDER GIN

20 oz. gin

0.1 oz. coriander
seeds

0.2 oz.
lemongrass,
chopped

1. Place the ingredients in a mason jar and let the mixture steep for 48 hours.

2. Strain before using or storing. For best results, use within 2 weeks.

RED,
RED ROSE

COURTESY OF HUMBERTO FLORES

2½ oz. Cedar &
Nutmeg Gin

¼ oz. grenadine

¾ oz. fresh
grapefruit juice

½ oz. Luxardo
maraschino
liqueur

1. Place all of the ingredients in a cocktail shaker, fill it two-thirds of the way with ice, and shake until chilled.

2. Strain into a tumbler containing one ice cube.

CEDAR & NUTMEG
GIN

¼ oz. cedar shavings

4 whole nutmeg, crushed

20 oz. gin

1. Place the ingredients in a mason jar and let the mixture steep for 48 hours.

2. Strain before using or storing. For best results, use within 2 weeks.

SORREL & SPICE

COURTESY OF HUMBERTO FLORES

2½ oz. Sorrel-Infused Gin

½ oz. limoncello

¾ oz. fresh lime juice

¾ oz. Honey & Ginger Syrup

1. Place all of the ingredients in a cocktail shaker, fill it two-thirds of the way with ice, and shake until chilled.

2. Strain into a coupe.

SORREL-INFUSED
GIN

0.15 oz. dried sorrel

20 oz. gin

1. Place the ingredients in a mason jar and let the mixture steep for 48 hours.

2. Strain before using or storing. For best results, use within 2 weeks.

HONEY & GINGER
SYRUP

10 oz. boiling
water

5 oz. honey

5 oz. ginger,
peeled and
chopped

1. Place the ginger and honey in a mixing bowl and muddle to combine.

2. Add the boiling water to the mixture and stir until combined.

3. Let the mixture cool and strain before using or storing. The syrup will keep in the refrigerator for up to 1 month.

TEQUILA &
MEZCAL

CHIPOTLE MARGARITA

COURTESY OF DRIP BAR

GARNISH: 1 LIME WHEEL

Hawaiian black
salt, for the rim

2 oz. Chipotle
Mezcal

1 oz. fresh lime
juice

½ oz. agave
nectar

1 bar spoon of
Cointreau

1. Wet the rim of a cocktail glass and dip it into the salt. Chill the glass in the freezer.

2. Add the remaining ingredients to a cocktail shaker, fill it two-thirds of the way with ice, and shake until chilled.

3. Strain into the cocktail glass and garnish with the lime wheel.

CHIPOTLE
MEZCAL

1 (750 ml) bottle
of mezcal

4 dried chipotle
chili peppers,
chopped

1. Place the ingredients in a large mason jar and let steep for 48 hours at room temperature.

2. Strain before using or storing. For best results, use within 2 weeks.

PASCAL LOVES
MEZCAL

COURTESY OF ZACHARY SHARAGA & RAMI LEVY

GARNISH: 1 ORANGE SLICE DUSTED WITH CINNAMON SUGAR

¾ oz. Cinnamon-Infused Campari

¾ oz. Chile Puya Mezcal

¾ oz. Cocoa Nib Sweet Vermouth

1. Chill a Nick & Nora glass or a coupe.

2. Add the ingredients to a mixing glass, fill it two-thirds of the way with ice, and stir until chilled.

3. Strain into the chilled glass and garnish with the cinnamon sugar–dusted orange slice.

NOTE: This is a good cocktail to make a large batch of. Place 1 cup of spring water, the Campari, mezcal, and sweet vermouth and shake to combine. Place in the freezer for at least 4 hours before enjoying.

CHILE PUYA
MEZCAL

2 chile puya
peppers

1 (750 ml) bottle
of mezcal (40 to
45% ABV)

1. Add the chile puya peppers to the bottle of mezcal and steep for 3 hours.

2. Strain before using or storing. For best results, use within 2 weeks.

CINNAMON-INFUSED
CAMPARI

5 cinnamon sticks

1 (750 ml) bottle
of Campari

1. Add the cinnamon sticks to the bottle of Campari and steep for 8 hours, agitating the mixture every 2 hours.

2. Strain before using or storing. For best results, use within 2 weeks.

COCOA NIB SWEET VERMOUTH

4 oz. cocoa nibs

1 (750 ml) bottle
of sweet vermouth

1. Add the ingredients to a mason jar and refrigerate for 5 hours, gently shaking the jar halfway through. Refrigerating the infusion will keep too much bitterness from being extracted from the cocoa nibs.

2. Strain through a coffee filter before using or storing. For best results, use within 2 weeks.

PINEAPPLE EXPRESS

COURTESY OF HIDE BELOW

2 oz. Fortified
Pineapple Muscat

½ oz. Fino Sherry

1. Place the ingredients in a mixing glass, fill it two-thirds of the way with ice, and stir until chilled.

2. Strain into a Nick & Nora glass and garnish with a green olive skewered on a cocktail pick.

FORTIFIED PINEAPPLE
MUSCAT

2 cups Muscat

5 bay leaves

1 bar spoon
ascorbic acid

20 green
cardamom seeds

1 tablespoon
sugar

2 black
cardamom seeds

5 oz. Drouin La
Blanche Calvados

½ lb. pineapple
chunks

7 oz. Giffard
Caribbean
Pineapple liqueur

1. Place the Muscat and
   cardamom seeds in
   a blender and puree until
   smooth.

2. Transfer the puree to
   a vacuum bag, add the
   pineapple and bay leaves,
   seal, and cook sous vide at
   149°F for 1 hour.

3. Strain, stir in the sugar,
   Calvados, and liqueur, and
   use as desired. For best
   results, use within 2 weeks.

IT'S NOT EASY
BEING GREEN

COURTESY OF RABBITHOLE

GARNISH: 1 OLIVE

1½ oz. Arugula–
Infused Tequila

²/₃ oz. balsamic
cream

¹/₃ oz. agave
nectar

1 oz. fresh lime
juice

1. Add all of the ingredients to a cocktail shaker, fill it two-thirds of the way with ice, and shake until chilled.

2. Strain into a coupe and garnish with the olive.

ARUGULA-INFUSED
TEQUILA

1 cup arugula

4 cups tequila

1. Place the arugula in the freezer for 4 hours.

2. Place the tequila and the arugula in a vacuum bag, seal it, and sous vide at 140°F for 45 minutes.

3. Strain before using or storing. For best results, use within 2 weeks.

UMEBOSHI MARGARITA

COURTESY OF TRAVEL BAR

GARNISH: 1 LIME WEDGE

1½ oz. Shiso & Umeboshi Tequila

Juice from 1 orange wedge

½ oz. Caffo Solara Orange liqueur

1 oz. fresh lime juice

½ oz. simple syrup

1. Place the ingredients in a cocktail shaker, fill it two-thirds of the way with ice, and shake until chilled.

2. Strain over ice into a double Old Fashioned glass and garnish with a lime wedge.

SHISO & UMEBOSHI
TEQUILA

2 (750 ml) bottles of El Jimador Silver Tequila

6 fresh shiso leaves, bruised

12 umeboshi plums, halved and pitted

1. Place the ingredients in a large mason jar and store in a cool, dry place for 2 weeks, agitating the mixture occasionally.

2. Strain before using or storing. For best results, use within 2 weeks.

HERE'S
ME-GRONI

COURTESY OF BABEL

¾ oz. Ilegal
mezcal

¾ oz. Cointreau

¾ oz. Campari

¹/₃ oz. Chili &
Mango Shrub

1. Place all of the ingredients in a mixing glass, fill it two-thirds of the way with ice, and stir until chilled.

2. Strain into a rocks glass and add ice. Express the strip of grapefruit peel over the cocktail and then drop it in for garnish.

CHILI & MANGO
SHRUB

1 cup diced
mango

3 red chili
peppers, chopped

¾ cup apple cider
vinegar

¾ cup sugar

1. Place the mango, chili peppers, and vinegar in an airtight container and shake to combine. Seal and let stand at room temperature for 3 days, gently shaking the container each day.

2. After 3 days, taste and see if the flavor is to your liking. If it is not as strong as you'd like, re-seal the container and continue shaking and tasting each day until it is.

3. When the flavor is to your liking, strain and press down on the solids to extract as much liquid as possible. Place the strained liquid and the sugar in a saucepan and bring to a boil over medium heat, while stirring. Reduce the heat to low and simmer for 10 minutes. Remove from heat and let cool completely before using or storing. The shrub will keep in the refrigerator for up to 1 month.

GRAPE
MARGARITA

COURTESY OF MAISON FRANCOIS

Himalayan salt,
for the rim

2 oz. Casamigos
Blanco Tequila

¾ oz. Grape Soda
Reduction

1 oz. fresh lime
juice

1. Wet the rim of a coupe and coat it with the Himalayan salt. Place the coupe in the freezer.

2. Place the remaining ingredients in a cocktail shaker, fill it two-thirds of the way with ice, and shake until chilled.

3. Double-strain into the chilled coupe.

Maison Francois is a brand-new brasserie and wine bar in the heart of London's St. James's neighborhood. Inspired by the simplicity and seasonality that are hallmarks of Paris' brasseries, it manages to be both welcoming and chic.

GRAPE SODA
REDUCTION

1½ cups grape soda

5.3 oz. caster sugar

1. Place the soda in a saucepan and bring to a simmer over low heat.

2. When the liquid has reduced by half, stir in the caster sugar. When the sugar has dissolved, remove the pan from heat and let it cool before using or storing. The reduction will last for up to 1 month in the refrigerator.

TIGER STYLE

COURTESY OF HUMBERTO FLORES

½ oz. Agave & Palo Santo Syrup

2 oz. Tiger Nut & Palo Santo Tequila

½ oz. raspberry liqueur

½ oz. fresh lime juice

½ oz. fresh tangerine juice

1. Place all of the ingredients in a cocktail shaker, fill it two-thirds of the way with ice, and shake until chilled.

2. Strain into a coupe.

TIGER NUT & PALO
SANTO TEQUILA

1½ oz. tiger nuts

½ oz. palo santo shavings

20 oz. tequila

1. Place all of the ingredients in a mason jar and let the mixture steep in a cool, dark place for 48 hours.

2. Strain before using or storing. For best results, use within 2 weeks.

AGAVE & PALO SANTO
SYRUP

1/4 oz. palo santo
shavings

1 cup boiling
water

1 cup agave
nectar

1. Place the palo santo shavings and boiling water in a mixing bowl and let the mixture steep until it is room temperature.

2. Stir in the agave nectar and strain before using or storing.

THE
DAISY AGE

COURTESY OF HUMBERTO FLORES

2 oz. tequila

¹/₃ oz. fresh lime juice

½ oz. orange liqueur

½ oz. Guava Syrup

¼ oz. Campari

¹/₃ oz. fresh lemon juice

1. Place all of the ingredients in a cocktail shaker, fill it two-thirds of the way with ice, and shake until chilled.

2. Strain into a coupe.

GUAVA
SYRUP

5 or 6 whole guava

20 oz. water

10 oz. sugar

1. Place the guava and water in a saucepan and bring to a boil. Boil for 10 minutes, remove the pan from heat, and let the mixture cool slightly.

2. Lightly mash the guava, stir in the sugar, and return the mixture to a boil, stirring to dissolve the sugar.

3. Cook until reduced by half, strain, and let cool before using or storing. The syrup will keep in the refrigerator for up to 1 month.

SMOKE & YELLOW
ROSES

COURTESY OF HUMBERTO FLORES

2 oz. Cedar-
Infused Tequila

½ oz. simple
syrup (made with
demerara sugar)

¾ oz. Yellow
Chartreuse

1 oz. Passion Fruit
Puree

½ oz. fresh yuzu
juice

1. Place all of the ingredients in a cocktail shaker, fill it two-thirds of the way with ice, and shake until chilled.

2. Strain into a coupe.

CEDAR-INFUSED TEQUILA

1½ oz. cedar shavings

20 oz. tequila

1. Place the ingredients in a mason jar and let the mixture steep for 48 hours.

2. Strain before using or storing. For best results, use within 2 weeks.

RUN
DEEP

COURTESY OF ZACHARY SHARAGA & RAMI LEVY

2 oz. Chamomile
Rhum Agricole

¾ oz. Acai Honey

¾ oz. fresh lime
juice

¾ oz. Grapefruit
Aquafaba

1. Chill a coupe.

2. Place all of the ingredients in a cocktail shaker, fill it two-thirds of the way with ice, and shake until chilled.

3. Double-strain into the chilled coupe and garnish with the Peychaud's Bitters and lime zest.

> **GRAPEFRUIT AQUAFABA:** Place 2 oz. ruby red grapefruit zest and ½ cup aquafaba in a mason jar and refrigerate for 1½ hours. Strain before using or storing. This will keep in the refrigerator for up to 2 weeks.

CHAMOMILE RHUM
AGRICOLE

4 bags of quality chamomile tea

1 (750 ml) bottle of rhum agricole

1. Add the ingredients to a jar, gently shake to combine, and steep for 1½ hours.

2. Remove the tea bags before using or storing. For best results, use within 2 weeks.

ACAI
HONEY

¹/₃ cup clover
honey

¹/₃ cup
unsweetened acai
puree, thawed

1. Add the ingredients to a mason jar and shake until combined.

2. Strain before using or storing. The honey will keep indefinitely.

LONDON HAZE

COURTESY OF KEYSTONE CRESCENT

GARNISH: 1 LIT CEDAR WRAP

1 oz. Pineapple
Sailor Jerry

¾ oz. Monin
Vanilla Syrup

1 oz. Cana Brava
3-Year-Old Rum

1 oz. passion fruit
puree

¾ oz. fresh
lime juice

1. Place all of the ingredients in a cocktail shaker, fill it two-thirds of the way with ice, and shake until chilled.

2. Double-strain over ice into a tumbler. Garnish with the lit cedar wrap.

> Located in the rapidly developing neighborhood of North London, Keystone Crescent is a cozy members-only lounge willing to turn over all stones for inspiration. Here, bartender Dimitris Gryparis looked back to 1952, when air pollution shut down London for four days and caused significant health issues.

PINEAPPLE SAILOR
JERRY

1 (750 ml) bottle
of Sailor Jerry rum

10.5 oz. chopped
pineapple

1. Place the ingredients in a large mason jar and store it in the refrigerator for 1 week.

2. Strain before using or storing. For best results, use within 2 weeks.

OBSIDIAN

COURTESY OF COUPETTE

1⅓ oz. Bacardi
Ocho rum

3 dashes of
chocolate bitters

⅓ oz. Cocchi
Barolo Chinato

1 bar spoon Amer
Picon

⅓ oz. Passion
Fruit Cordial

1. Place all of the ingredients in a mixing glass, fill it two-thirds of the way with ice, and stir until chilled.

2. Strain into a coupe.

PASSION FRUIT
CORDIAL

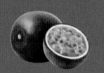

7 oz. passion fruit, chopped

2½ cups simple syrup

2 bar spoons of citric acid

1. Place the ingredients in a vacuum bag, seal it, and cook it sous vide at 149°F for 3 hours.

2. Strain before using or storing. The cordial will keep in the refrigerator for up to 1 month.

KING CAKE
DAIQUIRI

COURTESY OF COREY LITTLEFIELD

GARNISH: DECORATIVE PURPLE, YELLOW & GREEN SUGARS OR PEYCHAUD'S BITTERS

1½ oz. King Cake–
Infused Rum

1 egg

¾ oz. fresh lime
juice

½ oz. simple syrup

½ oz. Peychaud's
Aperitivo liqueur

1. If using the decorative sugars for garnish, wet the rim of a coupe and dip it into the sugars in the desired design.

2. Place the ingredients in a cocktail shaker, fill it two-thirds of the way with ice, and shake until chilled.

3. Strain the cocktail, discard the ice from the shaker, and place the cocktail back in the shaker. Dry shake for 15 seconds, strain it into the coupe, and garnish with the bitters, if using.

KING CAKE-INFUSED
RUM

1 king cake

1 cup brown sugar

1 (750 ml) bottle
of El Dorado
5-Year-Old Rum

1. Cut the king cake into quarters and place them in a large mason jar.

2. Add the brown sugar and rum and gently muddle the ingredients until combined. Cover and refrigerate for 48 hours.

3. Strain before using or storing. Store in the refrigerator and shake before using. For best results, use within 2 weeks.

HONEY BUZZ MILK
PUNCH

COURTESY OF LAURA BELLUCCI/BELLE EPOQUE

1½ oz. Honey Nut Rum

½ oz. honey syrup

2 oz. half & half

1 to 2 drops of El Guapo Holiday Pie Bitters

1. Place all of the ingredients in a cocktail shaker, fill it two-thirds of the way with ice, and shake until chilled.

2. Strain over ice into an Old Fashioned glass.

HONEY NUT
RUM

4 cups Honey Nut
Cheerios

White rum, as
needed

1. Fill a 1-quart mason jar with the cereal and then add rum until it reaches the brim. Cover and refrigerate for 24 hours.

2. Strain through cheesecloth before using or storing. For best results, use within 2 weeks.

DATE WITH
THE NIGHT

COURTESY OF HUMBERTO FLORES

GARNISH: 1 LEMON TWIST

---

2 oz. Date &
Walnut Rum

½ oz. fresh grape
juice

½ oz. damiana
liqueur

¼ oz. maple syrup

½ oz. Cherry
Heering

½ oz. fresh lime
juice

1. Place all of the ingredients in a cocktail shaker, fill it two-thirds of the way with ice, and shake until chilled.

2. Strain over ice into an Old Fashioned glass.

DATE & WALNUT
RUM

5 oz. dates

4 oz. walnuts,
crushed

20 oz. rum

1. Place the ingredients in a large mason jar and let the mixture steep for 48 hours.

2. Strain before using or storing. For best results, use within 2 weeks.

PAINT THE
TOWN RED

COURTESY OF HUMBERTO FLORES

2 oz. Hibiscus & Magnolia Rum

½ oz. fresh blood orange juice

1 oz. Aperol

½ oz. Hibiscus Syrup

½ oz. crème de cassis

½ oz. fresh lemon juice

1. Place all of the ingredients in a cocktail shaker, fill it two-thirds of the way with ice, and shake until chilled.

2. Strain over ice into an Old Fashioned glass.

HIBISCUS &
MAGNOLIA RUM

0.2 oz. dried
hibiscus

0.2 oz. magnolia
berry vine seeds

20 oz. rum

1. Place the ingredients in a mason jar and let the mixture steep for 48 hours.

2. Strain before using or storing. For best results, use within 2 weeks.

HIBISCUS
SYRUP

1 cup water

2 tablespoons
loose-leaf
hibiscus tea

1 cup sugar

1. Place the water in a saucepan and bring it to a boil.

2. Remove the pan from heat, add the hibiscus tea, and let the mixture steep for 10 minutes.

3. Strain the tea into the saucepan, set the heat to medium, and add the sugar. Stir until the sugar has dissolved, reduce heat to low, and let the mixture simmer until it is a thick syrup.

4. Remove from heat and let cool completely before using or storing. This syrup will keep in the refrigerator for up to 1 month.

BRIGHTER DAYS

COURTESY OF HUMBERTO FLORES

2½ oz. Pomegranate & Rose Rum

Club soda, to top

¾ oz. Fernet–Branca

1 oz. apricot puree

½ oz. Honey & White Balsamic Reduction

1. Place all of the ingredients, except for the club soda, in a cocktail shaker, fill it two-thirds of the way with ice, and shake until chilled.

2. Strain over ice into a highball glass and top with the club soda.

POMEGRANATE &
ROSE RUM

Seeds of 1
pomegranate

0.05 oz. dried
rose petals

20 oz. rum

1. Place the ingredients in a mason jar and let the mixture steep for 48 hours.

2. Strain before using or storing. For best results, use within 2 weeks.

HONEY & WHITE BALSAMIC
REDUCTION

½ cup honey

½ cup white balsamic vinegar

1. Place the ingredients in a saucepan, stir to combine, and bring to a boil.

2. Boil until the mixture has reduced by half, remove the pan from heat, and let it cool before using or storing. The reduction will keep indefinitely.

WINES & LIQUEURS

SUNFLOWER CHARTREUSE
SPRITZ

COURTESY OF ARTESIAN

Dash of salt

1²⁄₃ oz. club soda

½ oz. Grey Goose
Vodka

1¼ oz. Sunflower
Chartreuse

1. Build the cocktail in a highball glass containing ice by adding the ingredients in the order they are listed. Stir until chilled.

SUNFLOWER
CHARTREUSE

7 oz. sunflower
seeds

½ oz. malic acid

27 oz. Yellow
Chartreuse

1 teaspoon lactic
acid

13½ oz. vodka

7 oz. sugar

1. Place the sunflower seeds in a dry skillet and toast over medium heat until golden brown, about 10 minutes. Shake the pan as the sunflower seeds toast to prevent them from burning.

2. Place the remaining ingredients in a vacuum bag, add the toasted sunflower seeds, and seal the bag. Refrigerate for 24 hours.

3. Strain before using or storing. For best results, use within 2 weeks.

POUGHKEEPSIE

COURTESY OF LAURA BELLUCCI/BELLE EPOQUE

1 oz. Chamomile
Vermouth

2 oz. Angel's Envy
Bourbon

2 dashes of
Bittermens Boston
Bittahs

1. Place all of the ingredients in a mixing glass, fill it two-thirds of the way with ice, and stir until chilled.

2. Strain over ice into a double Old Fashioned glass.

CHAMOMILE
VERMOUTH

1 (1 liter) bottle of Carpano Antica Formula Vermouth

2 tablespoons loose-leaf chamomile tea

1. Place the ingredients in a large mason jar and let the mixture steep at room temperature for 48 hours.

2. Strain before using or storing. For best results, use within 2 weeks.

KING CAKE
SUA DA

COURTESY OF LAURA BELLUCCI/BELLE EPOQUE

GARNISH: 1 PLASTIC KING CAKE BABY

Cake frosting, for the rim

1½ oz. King Cake–Infused Cognac

Sprinkles, for the rim

1 drop of pure vanilla extract

2 oz. freshly brewed espresso

10 dashes of St. Elizabeth Allspice Dram

1 oz. sweetened condensed milk

1. Place cake frosting and sprinkles in a shallow bowl and stir to combine. Dip the rim of a Collins glass into the mixture.

2. Add the espresso and sweetened condensed milk to the glass and stir until thoroughly combined. Stir in the remaining ingredients, add ice, and stir until chilled.

3. Garnish with the plastic king cake baby.

KING CAKE-INFUSED
COGNAC

1 king cake

2 (750 ml) bottles
of Cognac

1. Scrape all of the frosting and sprinkles from the cake. Tear the cake into small pieces, place them in a container, and then add the bottles of Cognac. Chill in a colder-than-average refrigerator for 2 days.

2. Line a fine sieve with coffee filters and slowly strain the Cognac mixture. Strain again through cheesecloth before using or storing. For best results, use within 2 weeks.

GRASS

COURTESY OF MACE

1½ oz. White Tea–
Infused Shochu

¾ oz. Grass
Cordial

1. Place the ingredients in a mixing glass, fill it two-thirds of the way with ice, and stir until chilled.

2. Strain over a large ice sphere into a tea cup and garnish with the wheatgrass.

Mace, located in New York's Greenwich Village, is one of many projects for drinks industry veteran Greg Boehm (he of Cocktail Kingdom fame). This particular cocktail showcases a white tea infusion which is then washed with milk to strip the tannins from the over-steeped tea, while keeping the flavor strong and in the forefront.

WHITE TEA-INFUSED
SHOCHU

2 teaspoons loose-leaf white tea

1 (750 ml) bottle of shochu

7 oz. soy milk

¾ oz. fresh lemon juice

1. Place the tea and shochu in a vacuum bag, seal it, and sous vide at 176°F for 7 minutes. Strain and set the liquid aside.

2. Combine the soy milk and lemon juice and gently swirl until the soy milk curdles. Add the infused shochu and gently swirl to combine.

3. Strain through cheesecloth until the shochu is coming through clear, making sure not disturb the curds. For best results, use within 2 weeks.

GRASS CORDIAL

1½ lbs. caster
sugar

2½ oz. wheatgrass
powder

57¼ oz. water

²/₃ oz. citric acid

2 teaspoons
tartaric acid

1. Place the sugar and water in a saucepan and bring to a simmer over medium heat, stirring to dissolve the sugar. When the sugar has dissolved, remove from heat and let cool.

2. Place the syrup and the remaining ingredients in a blender and puree until combined. The cordial will keep in the refrigerator for up to 1 month.

LAVENDER

COURTESY OF MACE

1½ oz. Brown
Butter & Tonka
Cognac

¾ oz. Blueberry
Lavender Shrub

½ oz. verjus

1 oz. Champagne

1. Chill a coupe in the freezer.

2. Place the Cognac, shrub, and verjus in a Boston shaker, add 5 ice cubes, and shake until chilled.

3. Double-strain into the chilled coupe, top with the Champagne, and gently stir once with a bar spoon.

4. Garnish with the sprig of lavender, laying it across the top of the coupe.

BROWN BUTTER &
TONKA COGNAC

1 (750 ml) bottle of Cognac

2 tonka beans

2 tablespoons unsalted butter, browned

1. Place all of the ingredients in a mason jar and let them steep for 1 hour, stirring occasionally.

2. Place the mason jar in the freezer and freeze until the butter has solidified.

3. Scrape off the butter and discard it. Strain the liquid through a coffee filter before using or storing. For best results, use within 2 weeks.

BLUEBERRY LAVENDER
SHRUB

4¼ lbs.
blueberries

4¼ lbs. sugar

²/₃ oz. dried
lavender

Balsamic vinegar,
as needed

1. Place the blueberries, sugar, and dried lavender in a saucepan and simmer over low heat for 10 minutes.

2. Strain, pressing down on the berries to extract as much of their juice as possible.

3. Measure the amount of liquid and add one-third that amount of balsamic vinegar. Stir and use as desired. The shrub will keep in the refrigerator for 1 month.

CROATIAN
COFFEE
COURTESY OF BARREL PROOF

GARNISH: FRESHLY WHIPPED CREAM & GRATED FRESH NUTMEG

---

4 to 6 oz. freshly brewed coffee

1 tablespoon brown or demerara sugar

1½ oz. Cacao-Infused Slivovitz, warmed

½ oz. Butter-Washed Armagnac

1. Place the coffee and sugar in a warmed Irish Coffee glass and stir to combine. Stir in the slivovitz and Armagnac.

2. Top with the whipped cream and grate nutmeg over the cocktail.

> Tucked away in the Lower Garden District of New Orleans, Barrel Proof is a typical neighborhood bar that unassumingly carries one of America's best whiskey collections, in addition to innovative cocktails like this.

CACAO-INFUSED
SLIVOVITZ

1 oz. cacao nibs

1 (750 ml) bottle
of slivovitz

1. Place the cacao nibs in a dry skillet and toast over medium heat, shaking the pan frequently, until extremely fragrant, about 10 minutes.

2. Place the toasted cacao nibs and the slivovitz in a large mason jar and steep at room temperature for 48 hours. Strain before using or storing. For best results, use within 2 weeks.

BUTTER-WASHED
ARMAGNAC

1¹/₃ oz. unsalted
butter, melted

1 (750 ml) bottle
of XO Armagnac

1. Place the butter and Armagnac in a large mason jar, cover it, and shake to combine.

2. Place the jar in the freezer overnight.

3. Remove the layer of butter and strain the Armagnac through cheesecloth or coffee filters before using or storing in the refrigerator, where it will keep for about 2 days.

Blue Phoenix is a Vietnamese-style rice wine produced in the US. The brand uses sticky rice to create a unique flavor that is both sweet and savory. This complexity makes Blue Phoenix a hit in cocktails, as you'll see when trying the following recipes.

PHO
COCKTAIL

COURTESY OF BLUE PHOENIX

GARNISH: FRESH MINT LEAVES

1 oz. Pho-Infused
Blue Phoenix

3 drops of
sriracha

1 oz. triple sec

1 oz. fresh lime
juice

2 drops of fish
sauce

1. Place all of the ingredients in a cocktail shaker, fill it two-thirds of the way with ice, and shake until chilled.

2. Strain the cocktail over ice into a tumbler and garnish with the mint leaves.

PHO-INFUSED BLUE
PHOENIX

1 (375 ml) bottle
of Blue Phoenix

3 cardamom pods

1 cinnamon stick

1 star anise pod

1. Place all of the ingredients in a mason jar and refrigerate for 5 days.

2. Strain before using or storing. For best results, use within 2 weeks.

SAIGON MULE

COURTESY OF BLUE PHOENIX

GARNISH: 1 LIME WHEEL

½ oz. fresh lemon juice

2 slices of fresh ginger

1 sprig of fresh mint

½ oz. Lemongrass Syrup

1 oz. Blue Phoenix

3 oz. ginger beer

1. Add the lemon juice, ginger, mint, and syrup to a copper mug and muddle.

2. Fill the glass with ice, add the Blue Phoenix and ginger beer, and stir until chilled and well combined.

LEMONGRASS
SYRUP

½ oz. fresh
lemongrass, sliced

1 cup water

1 cup sugar

1. Place all of the ingredients in a saucepan and bring to a boil over medium-high heat, stirring to dissolve the sugar.

2. Reduce the heat to medium-low and simmer for 5 minutes.

3. Remove from heat and let the syrup cool completely. Strain before using or storing. The syrup will keep in the refrigerator for up to 1 month.

VIETNAMESE MARGARITA

COURTESY OF BLUE PHOENIX

GARNISH: 1 LIME WHEEL

Sea salt, for the rim

2 drops of fish sauce

1 oz. Blue Phoenix

Pinch of lime zest

3 oz. Sour Mix

½ oz. fresh lime juice

1. Wet the rim of a Margarita coupe and dip it in the sea salt.

2. Place all of the remaining ingredients, except for the lime zest, in a cocktail shaker, fill it two-thirds of the way with ice, and shake until chilled.

3. Strain the cocktail into the coupe, sprinkle the lime zest on top, and garnish with the lime wheel.

SOUR MIX

1. Place the sugar and water in a saucepan and bring to a boil, stirring until the sugar has dissolved. Remove from heat and let cool.

2. Add the lemon juice and lime juice to the syrup and stir to incorporate. Use immediately or store in the refrigerator. The sour mix will keep in the refrigerator for up to 1 month.

1 cup sugar

1 cup water

1 cup fresh lemon juice

½ cup fresh lime juice

THE BEE'S
TEAS

COURTESY OF BLUE PHOENIX

GARNISH: ANGOSTURA BITTERS & 1 CHRYSANTHEMUM BLOSSOM

---

1 oz. Blue Phoenix

1 egg white

1 oz. honey syrup

½ oz. black tea

½ oz.
chrysanthemum
tea

1. Place all of the ingredients in a cocktail shaker and dry shake for 15 seconds. Fill the shaker two-thirds of the way with ice and shake until chilled.

2. Strain the cocktail into a Nick & Nora glass and garnish with the Angostura Bitters and chrysanthemum blossom.

> **NOTE:** To make honey syrup, simply substitute honey for the sugar in a standard simple syrup.

BETWEEN THE DEVIL & THE DEEP BLUE SEA

COURTESY OF SUGAR MONK

GARNISH: 1 STRIP OF LEMON PEEL

1½ oz. Baharat–Infused Aquavit

½ oz. fresh yuzu juice

½ oz. fresh lime juice

½ oz. Patchouli Syrup

1 oz. Tamarind Syrup

Brennivin Aquavit, to mist

½ oz. Vicario Monk's Secret liqueur

1. Place all of the ingredients, except for the Brennivin Aquavit, in a cocktail shaker, fill it two-thirds of the way with ice, and shake until chilled.

2. Mist a rocks glass containing an ice sphere with the Brennivin Aquavit and double-strain the cocktail into the glass. Express the strip of lemon peel over the cocktail and then use it as a garnish.

BAHARAT-INFUSED
AQUAVIT

2 teaspoons
Baharat Blend

1 (750 ml) bottle
of aquavit

1. Add the spice blend to the aquavit, seal, and let the mixture steep for 24 hours.

2. Double-strain before using or storing. For the best results, use this infusion within 1 week.

BAHARAT BLEND: Combine 5 tablespoons mild paprika, ¼ cup finely ground black pepper, 3 tablespoons cumin, 2 tablespoons coriander, 2 tablespoons cinnamon, 2 tablespoons ground cloves, 2 tablespoons ground rosehip, 1 tablespoon cardamom, 1 tablespoon ground star anise, and 1 tablespoon ground nutmeg. The blend will keep in an airtight container for up to 6 months.

TAMARIND
SYRUP

1 lb. tamarind
pods

2 cups water

2 cups sugar

1.   Remove the shells from the tamarind pods, finely chop the pulp, and set it aside.

2.   Place the water and sugar in a saucepan and bring to a boil over medium-high heat, stirring to dissolve the sugar. When the sugar has dissolved, add the tamarind and bring to a boil. Reduce the heat to medium-low and let the mixture simmer for 2 minutes.

3.   Remove the pan from heat and let it steep for 30 minutes. Strain through a fine sieve, pressing down on the tamarind to remove as much juice as possible.

4.   Discard the solids and strain the liquid again before using or storing. The syrup will keep in the refrigerator for up to 1 month.

PATCHOULI SYRUP

1 cup sugar

1 cup water

2 teaspoons
loose-leaf
patchouli tea

1. Place all of the ingredients in a saucepan and bring to a boil, stirring to dissolve the sugar. Let the mixture boil for 1 minute, remove the pan from heat, and let it steep for 30 minutes.

2. Double-strain before using or storing. The syrup will keep in the refrigerator for up to 1 month.

CUP OF COFFEE

COURTESY OF ARTESIAN

¹/₃ oz. simple syrup

2 oz. Cognac &
Green Coffee
Distillate

1. Place the ingredients in an Old Fashioned glass with ice and stir until combined.

COGNAC & GREEN COFFEE
DISTILLATE

6 cups Cognac

7 oz. green coffee beans

Water, as needed

1. Place the Cognac and the coffee beans in a vacuum bag, seal it, and let the mixture steep at room temperature for 5 hours.

2. Place the liquid in a rotavap and distill at 38°F and 30 mbar until nothing comes out.

3. Weigh the rejects and then discard them. Multiply the weight of the rejects by 1.5 and then add that amount of water to the distillate. The distillate will keep indefinitely.

STEP IN
TIME

COURTESY OF COUPETTE

1 teaspoon
Mandarin Essence

3 oz. club soda,
to top

1 oz. Mandarin
Leaf Cordial

½ oz. Grey Goose
Orange Vodka

1²/₃ oz. Sauvignon
Blanc

1. Place all of the ingredients, except for the club soda, in a mixing glass, fill it two-thirds of the way with ice, and stir until chilled.

2. Strain over ice into a Collins glass and top with the club soda.

MANDARIN LEAF
CORDIAL

21 oz. caster sugar

1/3 oz. citric acid

14 oz. water

20 mandarin orange leaves

1¾ oz. Mandarin Essence

4 mandarin orange peels

1. Place all of the ingredients, except for the mandarin orange leaves, in a saucepan and warm over medium heat, while stirring to dissolve the sugar. Cook for 10 minutes.

2. Place the mandarin leaves in a large mason jar and pour the syrup over them. Cover the jar and refrigerate for 24 hours.

3. Strain before using or storing. The cordial will keep in the refrigerator for up to 2 months.

MANDARIN ESSENCE: Place 7 oz. of strained fresh mandarin juice and 1 cup caster sugar in a saucepan and bring to a boil over medium heat, stirring to dissolve the sugar. Cook until reduced by half and use as desired.

ALPINE
VESPER

COURTESY OF LAURA BELLUCCI/BELLE EPOQUE

¾ oz. gin

2 dashes of
orange bitters

¾ oz. potato
vodka

¾ oz. Cocchi
Americano

½ oz. Christmas
Tree Absinthe

1. Add all of the ingredients to a mixing glass, fill it two-thirds of the way with ice, and stir until chilled.

2. Strain into a coupe or a cocktail glass.

CHRISTMAS TREE
ABSINTHE

¼ cup needles
from Christmas
tree

25 oz. absinthe
(136 proof or
higher)

1. Wash the needles in a solution of water and a few drops of white vinegar.

2. Strain, place them in a mason jar, and add the absinthe. Let steep for 10 days.

3. Strain before using or storing. For best results, use within 2 weeks.

FIVE GRAPE
LONG ISLAND
COURTESY OF THE COCKTAIL TRADING CO.

1 part Hennessy
Cognac

2 parts Acidifed
Sencha-Infused
Riesling Vermouth

1 part Comte de
Lauvia Armagnac

1 part El
Gobernador Pisco

1 part Nardini
Grappa

1. Place all of the ingredients in a highball glass with ice and stir until combined and chilled.

ELLIOT BALL: "The classic Long Island Iced Tea is the subject of modern notoriety, known to be something of a dog's dinner of a cocktail. There is, however, absolutely no reason why five spirits with affinity can't be mixed well together. In this case, we wanted to retain the main positive quality of the Long Island Iced Tea, that is, its playfulness—thus the drink is quite concentrated, and heavily carbonated in-house by us, allowing it to be bottled for consistency, then poured over ice to loosen up. The infusion in question involves Riesling vermouth and a cold-brew sencha tea, imparting a delightful herbal astringency to the finish of the drink, allowing it to have a rich, full body without feeling overly sweet."

ACIDIFED SENCHA-INFUSED RIESLING
VERMOUTH

1 (750 ml)
Belsazar Riesling
Vermouth

2 tablespoons
loose-leaf sencha
tea

1 oz. citric acid

1. Place all of the ingredients in a large mason jar and steep at room temperature for 24 hours.

2. Strain before using or storing. For best results, use within 2 weeks.

JAPANESE PEQUOT
FIZZ

COURTESY OF JEWEL OF THE SOUTH

GARNISH: 3 PELLETS OF GUNPOWDER TEA

2 oz. Gunpowder-
Infused Shochu

1 egg white

¾ oz. fresh lime
juice

½ oz. simple syrup

6 sprigs of fresh
mint

1. Place all of the ingredients in a cocktail shaker and dry shake for 15 seconds.

2. Fill the shaker two-thirds of the way with ice and shake until chilled.

3. Strain the cocktail into a highball glass and garnish with the gunpowder tea.

Jewel of the South is the creation of Chris Hannah, one of the best bartenders in New Orleans (and, truth be told, the United States). Chris was the long-time head bartender at the James Beard Award–winning Arnaud's French 75 Bar. He has since gone on to open two bars of his own, Manolito and Jewel of the South.

GUNPOWDER-INFUSED
SHOCHU

1 (750 ml) bottle
of shochu

2 tablespoons
loose-leaf
gunpowder tea

1. Place the shochu and tea in a large mason jar and let the mixture steep for 2 hours, agitating the mixture occasionally.

2. Strain before using or storing. For best results, use within 2 weeks.

POSTSCRIPT

2019 and 2020 have been a period filled with loss. Both for me personally—I lost my beloved mother, Hilma Maitland, to cancer in 2019—and for the world with the emergence of Covid-19 and the havoc that has ensued. As I write these words, the final social and economic toll will not be known.

As it stands, nearly every facet of our lives will change in the coming years. Our relationship to work, friends, family, travel—all of which shaped this book—will be transformed by what is happening now. Others will cover those changes better than I ever could, but I do feel that the book is incomplete without an attempt to address the pandemic's impact on the drinks industry.

I could not have written either of my books without the input of numerous bars, bartenders, and industry professionals. They taught me everything I needed to know, and are responsible for much of what I've passed on to you.

So, with that in mind, let me tell you a story...

In 2011, I read about this bar that was, to my mind, deep in the bowels of Brooklyn. It was in Williamsburg. Even then, even though gentrification was already in full swing, if I mentioned Williamsburg to my mother, she would laugh at the idea of me going there. For her Williamsburg was frozen in amber, forever the void she knew during the late 1970s and early 1980s. I had been to Williamsburg plenty when I moved back to NYC in 2000, and went to some crazy loft parties where I saw some things I won't bother to describe in these pages, to protect the innocent, and the guilty, and myself.

Here is the description of Noorman's Kil from their website—I doubt, even with a lifetime devoted to the task, that I could describe it any better:

With a selection of over 400 whiskies, Noorman's Kil features one of the most impressive collections in NYC. Whiskey lovers of all kinds are sure to expand their palates here.

More than just a place for libations, Noorman's Kil hosts regular whiskey tastings and other events that spotlight the many facets of whiskey heritage. An assortment of gourmet grilled cheeses are on the menu to balance the belly and 12 rotating beers are available on tap along with other spirits for the non-whiskey inclined.

The bar's gut-renovated interior has been handcrafted by its four owners, who are alumni of Barcade and The Gutter. A salvaged 19th century bar paired with a mix of modern and traditional millwork and metal fixtures effuses a classic American spirit. Noorman's Kil also boasts a large, garden backyard.

The bar's name is derived from a creek that once flowed through northern Brooklyn. Noorman's Kil also references the importance of water in the distillation of whiskey, which when translated from the Gaelic term usquebaugh, means "water of life."

While I had plenty of other options for whisk(e)y that were much closer to where I lived, the charming description and obvious devotion meant that I was happy to head to Noorman's Kil one New Year's Eve—where I found my dream way to spend that particular evening: no cover, a champagne toast at midnight, and a bar that feels like a living room filled with your very best friends. It remains one of the best New Year's I've spent in NYC. And that evening was no fluke. The place had a great staff, great whisk(e)y selection, and an amazing space—who could ask for more from a bar?

So, it was with shock but not surprise that I got wind of their closing this year.

Again, from their website:

Dear whiskey drinkers,

Almost exactly 9 years ago we opened a bar that sold two of our favorite things: whiskey and grilled cheese. Turns out, there are a lot of you out there who like these things. We have such a deep gratitude for all of the people who created the NK community. It was a difficult decision, but we have decided it's time for us to finish our drinks and say goodbye for the last time. Thank you for all the memories and unbelievable support over the years!

Best,

Gary, Billy, Marcel & Harold

In my mind's eye, Noorman's will always be open, and I'll be scanning their shelves for one more dram before I head home. But the reality is that it won't be the last bar you or I lose in the times to come. I'll thank the team in person when I see them, but felt that they deserved it in print as well.

Gentlemen—a heartfelt thanks from me to you for all the good times you provided me and my friends over the years.

I'm not going to run off a list of the bars and restaurants in NYC or elsewhere that are closing up shop. It wouldn't be complete by the time you read this, and, in all honesty, it hurts me to even have to think about it.

What I'd like to say is this: Thanks to all of the bars and bartenders that helped me with both of my books. I couldn't have done it without you.

I would also like to thank those that just took their time and effort to create amazing drinks for me and their patrons. And what I'd like to ask you the reader to do (even if you've now become a home bartending master due to all of your pandemic-related practice) is to visit and patronize the bars that remain or the new ones that pop up wherever you go and wherever you live (once it's safe, of course). They need you and I'm sure they still have plenty of tricks up their sleeves.

I'd like to thank my family (especially my father Garvis Maitland, my sister, Renee Banks, and my only nephew, whose name I'll withhold for his own protection, and all my friends (especially EBE, DDG, and the crew at the MWC) for helping me through what has one of the roughest years I've had to face.

Finally, one last thank you to my late mother, Hilma Maitland, to whom this book is dedicated, and whom I can't thank enough. She was my biggest cheerleader and I will say that it won't be same without you and your hugs.

METRIC CONVERSIONS

US Measurement	Approximate Metric Liquid Measurement	Approximate Metric Dry Measurement
1 teaspoon	5 ml	5 g
1 tablespoon or ½ ounce	15 ml	14 g
1 ounce or ⅛ cup	30 ml	29 g
¼ cup or 2 ounces	60 ml	57 g
⅓ cup	80 ml	76 g
½ cup or 4 ounces	120 ml	113 g
⅔ cup	160 ml	151 g
¾ cup or 6 ounces	180 ml	170 g
1 cup or 8 ounces or ½ pint	240 ml	227 g
1½ cups or 12 ounces	350 ml	340 g
2 cups or 1 pint or 16 ounces	475 ml	454 g
3 cups or 1½ pints	700 ml	680 g
4 cups or 2 pints or 1 quart	950 ml	908 g

INDEX

IMAGE
CREDITS

ABOUT
THE AUTHOR

Kurt Maitland started his spirits journey with drams of Jameson in college, and has been exploring the world of spirits in general, and whiskey in particular, ever since. He lives in New York City and is the deputy editor of the popular The Whiskey Reviewer website, the curator of the Manhattan Whiskey Club, and the owner of Whiskey Selections. He is also the author of *Drink: The Ultimate Cocktail Book* and *Measure, Shake, Pour*.

ABOUT CIDER MILL PRESS BOOK PUBLISHERS

Good ideas ripen with time. From seed to harvest, Cider Mill Press brings fine reading, information, and entertainment together between the covers of its creatively crafted books. Our Cider Mill bears fruit twice a year, publishing a new crop of titles each spring and fall.

"Where Good Books Are Ready for Press"

501 Nelson Place

Nashville, Tennessee 37214

cidermillpress.com